Cover art:

"THE MEDICINE MAN" BY CHARLES RUSSELL

"The Medicine Man," which Russell considered one of his finest paintings, is an accurate depiction of the pipe keeper leading the tribal band across the Plains to a new camp. Note the pipe keeper's hair style: braided and looped across the forehead, and fastened at the back. Curly Head (Bull Lodge's son) wore his hair so when he was the last official keeper of the Feathered Pipe. In fact, Curly Head bore a striking resemblance to Russell's medicine man, as photographs testify. Although Russell once identified this group as Blackfoot, a tribe he often visited, he was well acquainted with most of the Montana tribes and a Gros Ventre influence is certainly possible. Several photographs of Russell on the Fort Belknap Reservation, taken in 1905 by Sumner Mattesen, belong to the collection of the Milwaukee Public Museum.

THE SEVEN VISIONS
OF BULL LODGE

as told by his daughter, Garter Snake

Gathered by Fred P. Gone

Edited by George Horse Capture

University of Nebraska Press
Lincoln and London

First Bison Book printing: 1992

Library of Congress Cataloging-in-Publication Data
Garter Snake, 1868–1953.
The seven visions of Bull Lodge / as told by his daughter, Garter
Snake; gathered by Fred P. Gone; edited by George Horse Capture.
p.   cm.
Originally published: Ann Arbor, Mich.: Bear Claw Press, c1980.
ISBN 0-8032-7256-1 (pbk.) ISBN 0-8032-2361-7 (cl)
1. Bull Lodge, 1802?–1886.
2. Atsina Indians—Biography.
3. Atsina Indians—Religion and mythology.
4. Atsina Indians—Rites and ceremonies.
I. Gone, Fred P.   II. Horse Capture, George P.
III. Title.   IV. Title: 7 visions of Bull Lodge.
E99.A87B854   1992
978.6'004973—dc20
91-41602   CIP

Reprinted by arrangement with George P. Horse Capture

The visual materials in this book and the information about them are
due to the generous assistance of Mr. Richard A. Pohrt of Flint, Michigan. The following items belong to the Chandler-Pohrt collection and
are reproduced by courtesy of Richard A. Pohrt: black-and-white photographs of Fred P. Gone, and of Garter Snake. The drawings of parfleche
designs used in this book are from A. L. Kroeber, *Gros Ventre Myths and
Tales* (N.Y., Museum of Natural History, 1907).

We are grateful to the Amon Carter Museum of Fort Worth, Texas for
permission to reproduce "The Medicine Man" by Charles M. Russell.
Thanks to Joe Zayek of the Flint Institute of Arts for photographing
the items from the Chandler-Pohrt collection. Special thanks are due
to Elmer M. Main of the Gros Ventre tribe and Bureau of Indian Affairs, Fort Belknap Agency, for his assistance in identifying the only
known photograph of Garter Snake.

Map by Monica Wellington.

∞

*This book is dedicated to
the White Clay People
of the Fort Belknap Reservation*

CONTENTS

Introduction by George Horse Capture   11

A Prefatory Note by Fred Gone   21

THE SEVEN VISIONS OF BULL LODGE   27

    1. Seven Visions on Seven Buttes   29

    2. From Warrior to Healer   59

    3. Medicine Man, Pipe Keeper, Father   78

    4. The Last Experience   89

THE STORY OF THE FEATHERED PIPE   103

Appendix: Garter Snake As Pipe Child   123

ILLUSTRATIONS

Garter Snake   *facing page 14*

Fred P. Gone   *facing page 15*

INTRODUCTION
ON BEHALF OF THE WHITE CLAY PEOPLE

This book is part of a larger effort of tribal cultural restoration. Few people realize the importance of such efforts because non-Indians are seldom aware of the needs behind them. If they do not themselves feel this kind of need, perhaps it is because they lack a viable, living heritage in this country. That is sad. But it is sadder still that Indian people must be caught up in a world not of their making. We find ourselves drifting helplessly in the melting pot, unable to adapt to a system where survival is linked to an ethic of frantic competition. Some of us become lost, without direction or goal. We need far more than this. We need to live from our own history. By understanding it and the people involved in it, we may see our present more clearly and prepare for the future. No one can do this for us. Because we must learn from ourselves, it must be a tribal effort. This is such an endeavor.

We are the A'aninin — the White Clay People of Montana. Many other terms have been used to designate our tribe, such as the Atsina, Mintarrees, Rapid Indians and Fall Indians, but they are wrong. Even the name we are "officially" known by, the Gros Ventres, is inaccurate. From the dawn to the sunset of time, we will always be the People of the White Clay.

Our history is long, hard and colorful. Long ago we were one with the Arapaho. In the early 1700's in North Dakota, the tribe divided, with the Arapaho moving southwest and the White Clay People moving northwest into Canada. There were many contacts with non-Indians over the following years, and a number recorded their experiences — Hendry (1754), Cocking (1772), Umfreville (1784), and Mackenzie (1789), to name a few. We journeyed north past the forks of the Saskatchewan Rivers, then moved west and became a part of the feared Blackfeet confederacy.

In 1793 we burned a fort, the South Branch House, on the south Saskatchewan. A year later we destroyed a fort on Pine Island, called Manchester House (on the main branch of the Saskatchewan). Heavy pressure from more numerous and better-

11

armed tribes forced us south to the Missouri by the first decade of the nineteenth century. Before moving permanently out of Canada, we destroyed another fort, the Chesterfield at the mouth of the Red Deer River, in 1826. The next few years found us fighting Mexican troops in the Cimarron area and trappers at Pierre's Hole in Idaho. We may have been the tribe that gave John Colter a run at Three Forks, Montana. Because of our ferocity, isolation and small number (we have never been more than 3,000), we have almost been ignored by historians. But we know our own story, and that is what is important.

Our traditional life style passed with the buffalo. In 1888 we were placed on the Fort Belknap Indian Reservation in north-central Montana, which we now share with the Assiniboine. Today we number about 2,100 and are struggling to survive as a distinct tribal entity.

For several years some of us have been involved in a cultural project whose purpose is to locate and research all historical information relating to our tribe. There is a tremendous need for this work. Our schools must have this material to teach our children, who must not experience the identity problems we had to endure. They must realize that they are not only Indians, but White Clay People, the best.

Our research project has had a modest success, although it is only beginning. At tribal expense, we have had the only good books on our tribe reprinted:the two volumes of *The Gros Ventres of Montana* by Regina Flannery (Catholic University of America, 1953), which have been made available to everyone from the reservation. A tribal language dictionary was located, revised and printed, and it is now available to the tribe. Hopefully it will stimulate the re-use of our own language. Other projects are under way but in need of funding. We are trying to establish a reservation museum, but the effort is halted because of a lack of funds. We must somehow move forward with this vital project. We *have* to.

Our research has turned up previously unknown photographs, articles and books throughout the world, as well as helpful personal contacts. After our small beginning, a grant was awarded by the Rockefeller Foundation allowing us to visit and photograph the actual sites of our history. We visited museums on the east coast where we could photograph our ethnographic material. In fact, this was the first time we saw our traditional art style, because the reservation has been stripped barren.

One of the most important sources of information we found was a footnote in an article which referred to W.P.A. material. As the lead was pursued, a fascinating story emerged, and I want to give some account of it here, primarily for the sake of other tribes who can also benefit from it.

I have some misgivings, however, about making public the existence of a rich source of tribal material. If you look around, you see countless books on the American Indian. But do the Indian people really benefit from any of them? It is doubtful. Some would say that any information the non-Indian public possesses about the Indian must contribute to the relationship between the two races. To some extent that is true. But the benefits to us have been extremely limited, if we think of what is possible if people really cared and wanted to help.

From the first, non-Indians took away our land, our art and religion, our very way of life, and we received nothing in return. Today most of these things are gone and we are poor. Yet non-Indians are still taking and giving nothing in return. Now they write books about us, they use our art styles and study our religion and philosophy, but they have no respect for the living people. They come to our reservations and communities to interview, study, diagram, photograph and record. Then they take all of this information away for their own uses. They locate old monographs on Indians and have them reprinted without any contact with or responsibility to the tribes involved. People have become Indian "experts" without ever having had an actual relationship with a living Native American. This is not right. We are still being exploited and we have very little left. When the time comes, these people will even take our bones.

When an author writes an Indian-related book, he should establish a relationship with the tribe involved. He should invite our opinion or assistance. When a work is completed, free copies should be given to the tribe, or at least a discount should be offered. Why don't these writers come out and visit us, and see how we live? They might learn something. This is only a part of the total picture, but what we are saying is clear: don't exploit us any more.

In 1935 the Works Progress Administration was established by Executive Order. The W.P.A. provided employment to approximately 8,500,000 people during the depression which began in

1929. Working closely with state and local governments, it conducted a variety of programs of public works and community services. Many of the unemployed found work building roads, airports, schools, libraries, playgrounds, and other public facilities across the country.

One of the lasting contributions of the W.P.A. was its writing project, which extended to the tribal reservations. A knowledgeable individual was selected from a reservation to collect and record tribal material. The reservation worker was paid by the word, and the end result was often very impressive. For at that time persons were still here who had first-hand experience with the buffalo Indians. Most of these people possessed an incredible amount of knowledge. And since they were the last ones to practice the oral tradition, they were well versed in the tribal ways.

When the W.P.A. was terminated in 1943, the information that has been recorded was put into a final form and duplicated. One copy was kept by the reservation worker, another was usually sent to the state archives, and an official copy was sent to Washington, D.C. Over the years most of this precious material has remained untouched and protected. Since tribes are now realizing their need for it, they are gradually drawing upon it for tribal purposes. Hopefully this trend will continue. This material belongs to the tribes and they are the ones who should benefit by it.

This book is an example of one such tribal effort. It is the story of Bull Lodge, who was a great warrior and medicine man of our tribe. It was told by his daughter, Garter Snake, a tribal member, and recorded by our reservation worker, Fred Gone, another tribal member. Finally it has been edited by this writer, who is also a tribal member. In diminishing degrees of importance, each of us has had a hand in bringing this tribal knowledge to this time and place. From beginning to end this relationship spans over 150 years.

The life of this great man is precious to us because it reaches far into the past, when things were better. It takes us back to the time when we were still free. Previously we could only read journals that tell of this. But now, if we listen hard, we can hear one of our own tell us the true story, the way it was long ago. I should add here that Indian names often become changed when they are translated. The main reason for this is that other languages tend to turn experience into abstract concepts. For example, if a man's

GARTER SNAKE (IN-NIETSE)

Photograph taken at Hays, Montana
in 1937 by Richard A. Pohrt

FRED P. GONE

*Photograph taken at Hays,
Montana in 1965 by his
daughter, Mrs. Bertha Snow*

name in his native language conveyed the fact that he was a skilled rider of horses, the translation might simply be "horseman" or "rider". Many of the present names of Indian people are different than they originally were. Thus Garter Snake, the narrator of this book, stated in reservation records that her father's name was Buffalo Lodge. His full name in our native language may have been Buffalo Bull Lodge or The Place Where The Buffalo Bull Lives. In any case he now has a prominent place in Indian history as Bull Lodge.

His story is similar to that of Crazy Horse of the Sioux. Both were great, uncompromising warriors and holy men. Both put the welfare of their tribe and their religion above everything else. Both lived in accordance with the ancient traditions in a dedicated, honorable manner, and they both have a special place in the hearts of all Indians. If we can guide ourselves by their examples, we shall not go wrong.

The lineage descending from Bull Lodge is impressive. According to Garter Snake, her father was called Buffalo Lodge and her mother was Pretty Kill. Her brothers were White Porcupine, Otter Robe, Curly Head and Long Hair. All were prominent in the religious and political affairs of the tribe and reservation. Although Garter Snake passed away on November 28, 1953,[1] the family still has many prominent descendants living on the reservation.

Life styles were vastly different long ago. One had to possess not only intelligence, but great physical prowess just to survive in the day to day struggle. In order to become a respected leader, one had to excel by seemingly superhuman efforts. It didn't come easy. Yet in spite of the numerous adventures and achievements of Bull Lodge, only those which deal with religion or "power" seemed to have been worthy enough to preserve. And as Garter Snake's narrative emphasizes throughout, his personal religious life is inseparable from the role of the Feathered Pipe in the tribe. For there are two very sacred objects among our people, the Feathered Pipe and the Flat Pipe, which is even older. Bull Lodge's intimate, life-long relationship with the former is the key to his own under-

---

1. According to reservation records, Garter Snake was born in 1868 north of the Big Bend on the Milk River near Malta, Montana. She was 85 when she died in 1953.

standing of his life. We are extremely fortunate to have his personal history of the Pipe's tradition as his daughter faithfully recounts it. (See the final section of this book.) As for those activities which Bull Lodge did not directly associate with his religious life, we must look elsewhere, and records are few.

There are no known photographs or drawings of Bull Lodge. Because of his stature as a holy man, his mark is not found on any treaties. He was above everyday affairs. Bull Lodge's ability as a warrior and holy man spread across the territory and became acknowledged by Indians and non-Indians both. Plenty Coups, the great chief of the Crows, told this story about him:

> The other time our people used fire I was seven years old (in 1855), and I remember what was said among the men. The Hairy Noses (Prairie Gros Ventres) got into our village to steal horses, and were driven out and surrounded in some willows not far from this place — just over there by the spring where Cuts-the-bear's-ears lives now. When daylight came they killed several Crows who tried to drive them out, and our warriors saw that something different had to be done. Thick grass grew among the willows, and at last the Crows set it afire. But when the flames drew close to the enemy, one of the Wise Ones sang his Medicine Song, putting the fire out with rain. I was too young to know much about it, and what I'm telling you now came to me from others who were older. I do know, however, that Bull Lodge, the Wise One who sang and made rain come, was a very powerful man. Our chiefs finally called the Kicked-in-the-belly clan to drive the Hairy-noses out of the willows, and after a desperate fight the thing was done. But I remember it cost more than it was worth.[2]

It is certain that other warriors had similar stories of this great man, but their words have been lost on the prairie wind.

During this early period, the Jesuit missionaries were making inroads into the various Montana tribes. This activity was led by Father DeSmet of St. Louis. These dedicated men lived and traveled like Indian people, and many of them weakened and left Indian country, for it was a hard, bitter life for them. As the

2. Linderman, Frank B., *Plenty-Coups, Chief of the Crows* (Lincoln, Neb., University of Nebraska, 1962), p. 298.

missionary's influence spread, it inevitably clashed with native religion, and altercations erupted.

The following incident has been recounted in many versions, but the basic facts remain the same. Since it involves one of the missionaries, the story was preserved in a nineteenth century Jesuit history:

> Toward the end of February, 1862, Father Giorda, while on his way with his interpreter to visit the Gros Ventres, met with quite an adventure. He fell in with a band of warriors of Bull Lodge's camp, one of the chiefs of the tribe, and both he and his companion were made prisoners. The latter, however, managed to escape. The marauders not only took away from the missionary horses and provisions, but stripped him of everything he had on his person to his undergarments. No sooner had the savages taken from him the cassock, than the red-flannel undershirt he had on caught their fancy, and this last piece of his wardrobe the Father had also to surrender to his captors. The one, however, to whose lot fell the red tunic, was considerate enough before putting it on himself, to give the missionary in exchange part of his own habilment, whose wealth was in its scantiness and the nature of which could hardly be described. It is stated that the thermometer at the Fort marked at the time forty degrees below zero, and in his clotheless condition good Father Giorda came near to freezing to death. He managed, however, to make his way to the presence of Bull Lodge, who, on hearing that he who stood before him in such non-apparel and half frozen, was a Black Robe, handed him a buffalo skin for a covering, A few hours later horse and saddle, together with some of the other articles, his cassock, breviary and a pair of blankets, were restored to the Father, but he was not permitted to remain in the camp. [3]

In the 1922 reprint of this history, a curious footnote was added:

> In some MS. notes, also before us, but not in Father Giorda's own hand, we find it stated that the leader of the war party who so ill-treated the missionary, 'died, as he had

3. Palladino, L.B., S.J., *Indian and White in the Northwest, or a History of Catholicity in Montana* (Baltimore, John Murphy, 1894), p. 177.

lived, like a devil'; but we have not come upon any par-
ticulars on this point.[4]
If we could know the full story of this extraordinary man, what a
tale it would be! Fortunately, it was not entirely lost, as were so
many of our things.

The W.P.A. reservation worker who recorded this material
was named Frederic Peter Gone. His Indian name was Many
Plumes. Yellow Teeth and Pine Sing were his father and mother.
He was born at Old Fort Belknap near Chinook, Montana in 1886.
He attended the government school at the new Fort Belknap
Agency, south of Harlem, and left in 1901. Afterwards he made his
home in the Hays district of Fort Belknap Reservation at the foot of
the Little Rocky Mountains, until he passed away on February 8,
1967.

Mr. Gone always had a deep interest in his culture and his
tribe. From the Glenbow Institute in Calgary, Alberta, Canada to
Washington, D.C., one can locate tribal cultural contributions of
Fred Gone. It was doubtless because of this dedication that he was
selected as the reservation W.P.A. worker. His life-long concern for
our culture enabled him to do an outstanding job in gathering
these stories. In some cases he was his own informant, with rare
information he had learned long before as a youth. The tribe owes
him a debt of gratitude for saving these precious things for us.

After locating this W.P.A. material five years ago, it has been
studied when the opportunity arose. The editing was kept to a
minimum in order to retain the honesty of the original, although
some revision has been made to improve the readability. As the
material was studied we were struck by the extraordinary empha-
sis placed on anything having to do with religion or "medicine" or
"power." The old-timers deeply believed what they said, and they
believed in supernatural happenings, for some of them were actual
witnesses of them.

Being born after the majority of our tribal customs and beliefs
disappeared, the present generations have not been exposed to the
ancient religion. Raised in the modern world as Catholics, the
traditional tribal ways seem foreign to us. We question them and
say, "Like the buffalo, it is gone." But now, after years of spiritual
wandering, we are beginning to look at the Old Ways with a new

4. Palladino, L.B., *Indian and White in the Northwest* (Lancaster, Pa.,
   Wickersham, 1922), p. 195.

perspective. Surely if they have lasted for tens of thousands of years, they must be at least as good as those of any other religion. Perhaps they are much better, because they are more natural and free. With these thoughts in mind, I made a "circle trip" to all the sacred buttes that are mentioned in this book.

The first stop was McCann Butte at the east end of the Bear Paw Mountains, which overlooks our present reservation. I was accompanied on the climb by two tribal members, Al and John Buckman. This volcano-shaped butte is 4,308 feet high. It is next to Miles Butte, named after General Nelson Miles, who was said to have seen Chief Joseph's group from there as they made their way north.

I strapped on a backpack loaded with cameras, film, compass, canteen and other equipment, and I charged up the steep slope to find things out for myself. After five minutes of hard climbing, it occurred to me that it was not going to be that easy. Ten minutes later I placed my backpack under a rock and the climb continued. My heart began to pump frantically. I realized that no one would make that climb unless he were seeking something unobtainable elsewhere.

On top of that butte, you are on top of the world. Thousands of square miles lie below, stretching out in each of the four sacred directions. Looking down, with the wind blowing your mind clear of thoughts, you feel an unidentifiable presence there. The wind cleanses you, and you feel pure. You know you are in a holy place, holier than any church. You can *feel* God. The Old Timers prayed there for these reasons and more. These high solitary sentinels put them closer to The One Above and allowed them to *see farther* than they had seen before.

When my traditional duties were accomplished, I started down. The return trip was, if anything, more strained than the climb, because the angle put unused leg muscles to work. When I finally reached the bottom I felt shaky, but much better. I had learned something which will remain with me all my days, and I trust the future will complete it within me. When I return to the top of that butte, known to Bull Lodge as Last Butte, it will not only be for a longer time, but with a fuller partnership in the sacred circle of life. Everything the Old Timers believed is true. The power or "medicine" is still there, although we must look harder for it now. It is there on the buttes, but it is also alive in our hearts, waiting for us.

The rest of the tour of sacred buttes was completed without the feeling I experienced on McCann Butte. The other buttes had been invaded by the technological age. One has an electronic device installed at the top. Another is adjacent to a ski resort. Yet despite all the changes over the years, they stand as proud reminders of ancient Indian traditions.

Many people assisted with this book. I wish to thank Minnie Paugh of Montana State University for assisting with the original material; Sister Mary Claire of St. Paul's Mission, Hays, Montana; Madeline Colliflower and the staff of the C.A.P. Office and Roberta Swan of the College of Great Falls for helping with the typing. I am grateful to David Robbins and Karl Pohrt of Bear Claw Press for their assistance in the final stages of editing. And I am grateful to the Gros Ventre Treaty Committee for its support over the years and for travel funds for my circle trip to the seven buttes. We all feel an immense debt of gratitude to Mr. Fred Gone, who preserved this precious material for his people. The deepest thanks, of course, go to Bull Lodge, The Wise One, and to his daughter Garter Snake. We shall never forget.

This material belongs to the tribe, not to any individual. In order to commemorate this, the proceeds from this project will be used to establish a tribal education scholarship fund. Our present tribal structure precludes copyrighting this work in the name of the tribe. I have copyrighted it in my name on its behalf. This material must always be part of the White Clay People.

Working on this book has been a moving experience for me. It has opened my eyes to many unseen things. I shall try to pass them on to my children, as it was done in the past. But we can only introduce the concepts to the next generation. For like their fathers, they must find their own way within the bounds of tradition, and their hearts must be free to make this choice. Someday, if we are fortunate, they will climb their own buttes, completing the ancient circle.

George Horse Capture
Curator
Plains Indian Museum
Buffalo Bill Historical Center
Cody, Wyoming

ON THE HISTORY OF BULL LODGE'S LIFE AS TOLD BY HIS DAUGHTER, GARTER SNAKE WOMAN

By Fred P. Gone

The story of Bull Lodge's life, from his boyhood to the day he died, is directly connected with the history of the Chief Medicine Pipe which is called the Feathered Pipe. Frequently during the course of this story, we find mention of the supernatural powers given to Bull Lodge, who was chosen by the Chief Medicine Pipe to keep it for a certain length of time. These powers led to dream visions, magic, and many ways of practicing healing. They were inspirations to wisdom, foresight and leadership in the tribe, as was intended by the Chief Medicine Pipe. The life story of Bull Lodge enables us to understand these powers and how they worked. It shows us the true nature of the Gros Ventre medicine man. This account of Bull Lodge's life was told to me by his daughter, Garter Snake Woman. It is accurate, for she is gifted with an excellent memory. This is especially apparent in her reports of events where she herself was present—for example, in her descriptions of a few of the many medical cases which Bull Lodge treated.

Bull Lodge held the last sacred place in the history of the supernatural powers attached to the Chief Medicine Pipe, just as the Pipe itself had foretold at the beginning. Five men were chosen in sequence at the time of the origin of the Feathered Pipe. Later, four men were intended to receive its supernatural powers. Their lives were to be spaced widely apart in time, to cover a long period. Every sixteenth man was to receive the special powers attached to the Chief Medicine Pipe, until the fourth and last man received them. This was Bull Lodge. He served the Feathered Pipe better than any of the original owners, because he was the last to receive all its powers, which were added to those he had already received before he became a Chief Medicine Pipe Man. In this office he was extremely helpful to his people, as well as to the Crow tribe.

Since there are no longer any Gros Ventres living who can give an account of the supernatural powers of the Chief Medicine Pipe called the Feathered Pipe, this means of explaining them seems best. Also, it would be wrong to understand their working in terms of separate and scattered events. Bull Lodge's story presents these powers as they disclosed themselves gradually and continuously throughout a lifetime.

There were many medicine men with power, where it applied only to the single purpose for which it was granted. Others even had power for two or three purposes. But Bull Lodge possessed many far-reaching powers. He controlled rain and electrical storms. He was never known to lose a case in doctoring. He was widely known among neighboring tribes for his success in healing, which extended to hopeless cases of gunshot wounds as well as to the few sicknesses to which the Indians in those earlier days were subject.

It would require too much space to write down all the deeds of Bull Lodge which had a supernatural origin. There are many little incidents which have been remembered: like making rain when some families were forced to make a dry camp and the children cried for drinking water; like stopping storms, clearing the weather even when the spring equinox was at its worst; like making tobacco out of cottonwood bark, and making coffee, and finding cherries that were fresh in midwinter. Occasionally, when Bull Lodge was visiting tipis, the people would tell him they had no sugar to sweeten the tea and berry soup they wished to serve, and he would make sugar for them. He did not do these things habitually, but when his help was needed or when he was formally called upon, he would perform them. He was a dependable warrior because of the powers given to him for that purpose. But his greatest fame was as a healer. He was given the power to prevent death even when it was overtaking the afflicted person.

Since Bull Lodge's supernatural experiences began in the early period of his life, it is clear that his mind had always inclined him to become a great man of his tribe. His hardships of solitary fasting were numerous, and wherever he performed them, they were successful. Garter Snake Woman's story records the seven different places where he slept (that is fasted). There were also many other times of vision, apart from the seven fasts, where he was given supernatural powers. These experiences were not confined to one stage in his life. They began when Bull Lodge was twelve and continued, almost regularly, to the day he passed away[1]. The next seventy-two years of his life were controlled by the supernatural presences which the Indian of that day relied upon to help and protect him, and to guide his mind and heart to the Supreme Being.

Bull Lodge's final experience was to be his greatest. For he had been given the power of resurrection, and was in constant communication with "those who watch over him." However, the buffalo hides which had to be used for the sweat tent medicine ceremony could not be obtained, and the ceremony was not performed. The white man felt that the only way to settle our race was to kill off the buffalo which the Indian hunted for a living. So Bull Lodge passed beyond recall, calm and perfectly resigned to his fate.

For the remainder of this preface, I want to comment on several parts of this story which may not be clear to the reader. At the outset, for instance, we learn that Bull Lodge was a half-breed, and the reader might wonder how he regarded himself. We should consider this fact without prejudice. Bull Lodge's father was a Frenchman, known as High Crane in Gros Ventré but nicknamed Crooked Rump because he was hurt or deformed at the hip. His mother was a Gros Ventre woman named Good Kill. He never knew his father and his father never knew him. He was raised among his mother's people and always expressed a deep faith in their tradition, customs and habits. He became a great man among them despite the fact that his father was a white man and he was consequently born poor. Bull Lodge regarded himself as a hundred percent Gros Ventre. It was the only tongue he spoke, and he lived and died by it.

Now, the purpose of the story of Bull Lodge is to instruct us in the meaning of supernatural powers. Through the first part, while Bull Lodge is receiving these powers, we notice that he is not yet exercising them, and we might wonder why nothing is said about their use. At the completion of the story, however, we will understand how supernatural powers are meant to be used through an entire lifetime, and we should need no further explanation.

Garter Snake Woman tells us that Bull Lodge had revered the Chief Medicine Pipe called the Feathered Pipe from an early age. When the boy worshipped the Supreme Being through the Feath-

1. From reservation records and from Garter Snake's testimony, we know that Bull Lodge's birthdate was about 1802. He died in 1886. (GHC)

ered Pipe, it was fully in accordance with custom. We are shown how Bull Lodge would seek out the bed ground of the Feathered Pipe in the deserted camp area and place his hand upon it in supplication, and cry and pray. The word "crying," as it is used throughout these accounts, refers to a way of worshipping that has been handed down through the generations from the beginning. It is the outward act of calling down the attention of the Supreme Being upon the individual. After imploring the help of the Feathered Pipe, the Supreme Being appeared to Bull Lodge in the person of an old man. By the costume and by the way his face was painted, Bull Lodge immediately recognized him as a Medicine Pipe owner. This apparition meant that Bull Lodge was to become the owner of the Medicine Pipe. The old man's words are also significant. "Do you see my hair and robe, my sweat implement, how my face is painted? I give you all of this." This too could only mean that Bull Lodge would someday become the owner of the Medicine Pipe. Now, everything that is connected with the Medicine Pipe, or even that comes in contact with it, is held sacred by the Gros Ventre tribe. That is why young Bull Lodge chose to humble himself by crying on the bed ground of the Feathered Pipe and by holding his hands on the sacred place of incense.

Now in Bull Lodge's day the various tribes were constantly at war with one another. Considering the many times Bull Lodge was out by himself crying, placing himself at a disadvantage to the enemy, it is remarkable that he was never bothered by them. This testifies to the supernatural protection he was given throughout the years of his fasting experiences.

The buttes mentioned in the story, where Bull Lodge slept, were revealed to him as tipis in his visions. It will be noticed that all but one of the entrances are to the east, and that the importance of this direction is emphasized. The Indian always respects the east as the first direction, for the sun gives birth to the day there.

When we read of patients being operated upon with a woodpecker tailfeather to remove some object, we must understand this to refer to a tumor. This does not mean that it was the only possible use for the gift of the tailfeather, but that whenever necessary, Bull Lodge was to use it so in his surgical work.

Occasionally a certain phrase is heard in the story: "When you do this, I'll hear you." This means that the supernatural giver of some article will hear and recognize its special sound, whether it be a whistle, a song, a drum, or even a certain way of shouting. If the sound is made in a true way, exactly as it was told to be used, the giver will be present to insure success, whether the gift was intended as an implement for war or for doctoring or for any of the ceremonies which the Gros Ventre performed and lived by.

The reader may notice that the plants and roots which were given to Bull Lodge as medicines are not described here. Not all things can be made public. Some matters had to be omitted by the storyteller. The plants and roots used by famous doctors of the tribe, for instance, are never publicly revealed. This secrecy is a condition of receiving gifts supernaturally through hardships of fasting. Now all the rules pertaining to supernatural powers were strictly followed and held sacred by the Indian. To disregard them or to omit any from practice would be certain to bring severe consequences as well as loss of the gift itself. Therefore one who has received a supernatural gift must be very cautious about how much is publicly revealed. Almost all the medicine men, great and small, pass beyond with their secret still locked in their hearts.

Now of all the supernatural gifts, the most important are song, incense, the pipe filled with kinnikinnic, and prayer. In the story these four items are missing, because everything was written down exactly as Garter Snake Woman told it. Upon questioning her about these items when she had finished, she said they had indeed accompanied each and every gift that was given to Bull Lodge. So I am obliged to take this means of introducing them into the story.

Every gift Bull Lodge received was accompanied with song, incense, the pipe, and prayer. And whenever the time came for him to institute spiritual gifts into his life, they became part of his ceremonies. Thus each ceremony began with a song (given for a special purpose), incense (from some particular plant or root or leaf one is directed to use, in Bull Lodge's case the needles of the sweet pine tree), and the pipe and prayer, which are directly connected with each other. All four items must be used before, say, doctoring. First the doctor sings the song, then he makes the incense, then he takes the filled pipe and holding it up with both hands, the stem pointing up, he begins to pray. Thus song, incense and the filled pipe are elevated to the same position of ceremonial sacredness as prayer, and whenever the song and incense alone are mentioned here, it is understood that the pipe and prayer are also included.

A Note by Fred Gone

I have now commented upon this story of Bull Lodge's life the only way I know how. I hope what I have explained is clear. Most of what I have written here refers to the first part of this narrative, covering the years of Bull Lodge's youth. Then follow stories about those war experiences which were controlled supernaturally, then accounts of his work as a Medicine Man and doctor. In the final section, Garter Snake Woman tells of the last days of Bull Lodge's life on earth and of his death.

January 5, 1942
Hays, Montana

THE SEVEN VISIONS
OF BULL LODGE
as told by his daughter,
Garter Snake

THE PLACES OF THE SEVEN VISIONS
(GROS VENTRE NAMES IN CAPITALS)

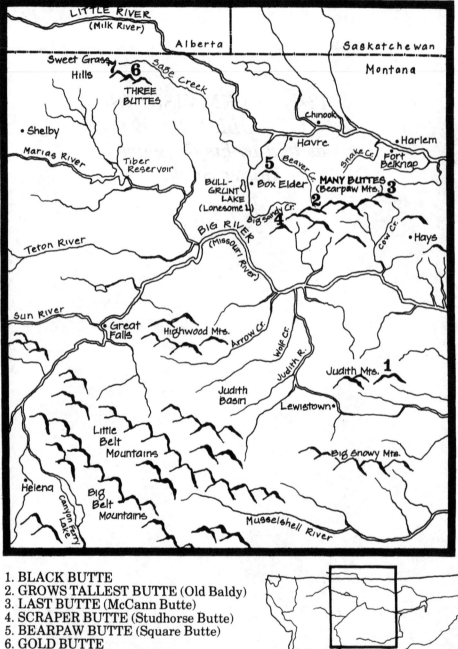

1. BLACK BUTTE
2. GROWS TALLEST BUTTE (Old Baldy)
3. LAST BUTTE (McCann Butte)
4. SCRAPER BUTTE (Studhorse Butte)
5. BEARPAW BUTTE (Square Butte)
6. GOLD BUTTE
7. PORCUPINE BUTTE

Montana

TERRITORY SHOWN ON THIS MAP

1. SEVEN VISIONS
ON SEVEN BUTTES

The Hudson Bay Company had a trading post on the upper Saskatchewan River, run by a white man whom the Gros Ventres called Crooked Rump. He was called this because he walked with a funny twist in that part of his body. He was the first white man with whom the Gros Ventre tribe had dealings, for they began to frequent the trading post then. This man, who was later called High Crane, married a young Gros Ventre woman named Good Kill and Bull Lodge came from this union. When the tribe moved away from that country, Good Kill left High Crane and lived with her relatives. The people moved south to country lying on both sides of the United States and Canadian border, including Montana, Alberta and the western part of Saskatchewan. I do not know exactly where my father was born. I only know that it was among his people, the Gros Ventres.

Visions of Preparation

When Bull Lodge reached the age of twelve, he knew he was motivated to become a great man of the tribe. Being poor, he had experienced hard times in his childhood. He began to consider how he could fulfill his ambition. Now through the later years of his childhood, he had a deep faith in and affection for the Chief Medicine Pipe which was called the Feathered Pipe. There were other medicine pipes in the tribe, but this one, the Feathered Pipe, was the pipe he chose to call upon as his guide and teacher. So he entrusted his life to it.

One day late in the spring of the year, as the tribe was breaking camp before moving, Bull Lodge wandered away from the others so that he would not be heard. He began to cry. He wandered about the country crying like a lost child. After this, he returned to the deserted camp grounds. Approaching the eastern side, he went from one tipi bed ground to the other, seeking out the tipi marks of the Chief Medicine Pipe which was called the Feathered Pipe. He discovered them by locating the shallow hole directly behind the fire place, where the live coals of buffalo chips are placed and the incense made. Also, he knew that the tipi of the Feathered Pipe must always face south. Starting at the entrance, he circled around the tipi. After making a complete circle he continued on until he reached the back. He knelt by the shallow hole in the ground where the incense was made, then he began to cry, keeping both hands over the hole in homage to the Feathered Pipe.

He remained in that kneeling position for a long time. When he stopped crying, he prayed to the Feathered Pipe to deliver him from his state of poverty. Then he continued to circle the deserted camp ground, crying as he walked. After reaching the point where he had started, he picked up the direction of the tribe's movement, noting the marks of tent poles and travois on the ground. But he did not cease his crying. Finally he said, "I wish there were someone up above who would have pity on me and help me to be a man so that I could live like a man." Each time the tribe moved, he did all these things.

One day after crying around the deserted campground, having followed the tracks of the moving tribe to a place where he was in sight of camp, his eye was attracted to a small coulee full of thick grass. It was so inviting that he lay down on the grass, looking up at the sky. He was tired from crying and walking, and he fell asleep. In his dream an old man approached, wearing a buffalo robe with the hair still on it. The robe was painted red where the old man's shoulders protruded. The waist line too had red paint going around the robe. The old man's long hair was matted, and in his hand he held one of the sweat bath implements, made of buffalo tail. His face was painted with the same dark red paint, exactly as a Chief Medicine Pipe owner paints his face.[1]

The tribe was moving in a northerly direction that spring and early summer, and Bull Lodge continued to wander off when the people were breaking camp. After they moved, he would return to the deserted campground and search for the bed of the Feathered Pipe. Standing at the extreme east of the campground, he would face west, holding his hands up in supplication to the Supreme Being. After praying, he would go from one bed ground to another. He would always begin by circling to the right, never to the left, continuing until he discovered the place of the Feathered Pipe. He would circle round it once completely to the right, to signify the way the Feathered Pipe was handled. Then he would continue to circle the tipi mark until he was directly opposite the entrance mark.

The tipi where the Feathered Pipe was kept must always face south, and the Medicine Pipe owner sits at the back end of the tipi, facing the entrance. After stopping in the place where the Medicine Pipe owner sits, Bull Lodge would kneel down and hold his hands over the hole where the incense is made, making his cries and prayers to the Feathered Pipe. Then he would complete his circle of the entire campground, going to the right in order to go towards the sun. Afterwords he would follow the marks left by the tribe when they moved. When he was in sight of the tipis, he would find some nice secluded spot and lie there until dusk before returning home. Bull Lodge had made it a rule that he could not enter the camp until dusk. And by his own choice he was fasting, for he included this duty in his way of seeking his future.

One day the old man who had appeared to him in his vision spoke to him.

"My child, why do you do these things? Why do you look for me

1. The owners of the Chief Medicine Pipe have a special way of painting their faces red: from temple to temple across the forehead, and on both lower jaws across the chin, with the paint ending about even with the ear lobe.

in particular, locating my bed ground in the deserted camp? My child, I have noticed this custom you have adopted for yourself, holding your hands on the place where the incense is made for me. And your cries have moved me with compassion.

"I pity you, my child. You will be powerful on this earth. Everything you have asked for is granted you. Now, my child, look at me. Do you see my hair, my robe, my sweat implement, and how my face is painted?

"I give you all of it. Are you sure that you recognize the robe?"

"Yes," Bull Lodge answered. The robe was the skin of a grizzly bear and the sweat implement was made from the tail of the white buffalo.

"I will give you something very soon, my child."

And Bull Lodge thought, "I am still just a boy, but this old man looks like a medicine man of the Chief Medicine Pipe. Clearly he belongs to the Feathered Pipe which I have chosen as my special guide, and whose incense place I hold my hands upon in the deserted campgrounds."

Then the old man disappeared, and Bull Lodge awoke. He sat up and looked about for the old man. Seeing that he was alone he said, "I wish that this thing which is coming to me might come right away." And as the day was almost spent, he returned to camp to his tipi.

Bull Lodge followed his customary ceremonies for three months, from late spring into the summer. Then one summer day, after he had finished crying around the deserted camp ground, having followed the tribe's tracks to his stopping place, he lay in the grass on his back with his arms out flat on the ground, elbows bent. He lay in that position for quite a while. As he gazed up at the sky, an object appeared, very small, but he could see that it was moving. It looked like a circling bird. He just lay there, watching that speck in the sky. Then it seemed to him that it was coming down in small circles. It came closer and closer, and the closer it came, the bigger it got, until it came within arm's length. It was a shield, with a string or fine cord attached to it leading up into the sky.

The shield hung suspended before Bull Lodge, as if giving him plenty of time to examine it and to imprint its features on his mind. It was about a foot and a half in diameter. The surface presented to him was painted half red and half dark blue. A painted rainbow went all around the edge. In the center a black bird was painted, and from each side of the bird's head, green streaks of lightning, ending at the rainbow's inside rim. Eagle feathers hung in a double row from the outside rim. In the center of the shield hung a single soft, fluffy feather.

The shield suspended itself a while for Bull Lodge's inspection, then it lowered itself the rest of the way until it rested upon him.

Then Bull Lodge heard a voice. The sound came from behind the shield, which was resting on his face and upper chest. He could not judge whether the voice came from directly behind the shield or from a little way off, but it was quite close to the shield.

"My child, look at this thing. I am giving it to you from above. It is for your living. In times of danger when you need my help, you must always say, 'Help me, Thunder Sing.' I will always hear you when you pronounce my name: Thunder Sing. Now I will instruct you concerning what you must do. There are seven buttes on this earth that you must sleep on. You must do this in imitation of me, for I too have done it.

"From this time on, everything you do will be good. Have you made sure that you have taken a good look at this thing I have presented to you?"

Bull Lodge, still lying on his back, answered "Yes" in his mind.

Then the voice said, "I command you to make one like it for your own use. Your instructions for the shield's use will be given to you later. I will always be watching you and guarding you from above."

Then the voice left, and the shield rose up from Bull Lodge's chest and gradually disappeared into the sky. For a while Bull Lodge just lay on the earth. Then he sat up. "A-ho," he said, "I am glad that my Father has given me a living." He remained there for a long time, pondering the event. Then he rose and went home.

He ate his supper, but he still felt restless. He was too excited to sit quietly, so he took up his robe and went back out away from the camp. He walked to the top of a nearby hill and lay there with his face down. His restlessness gradually disappeared and the quiet and peace of the night overcame him. And as he lay there he heard a voice above him.

"I was sent with a message to you from your Father. You are to go to a particular butte called Black Butte, which stands out away from these mountains to the east.[2]

"On this butte, which stands on the south side of the Big River (the Missouri), you are to stay and fast for seven days and nights. Before you start out to the designated fasting place, it will rain. That will signify your purification."

Bull Lodge lay there for a while without stirring. Then, since nothing else happened, he sat up and looked around. It was dark and peaceful. Since he did not notice anything unusual, he arose and went back to camp.

All the while he was returning, he was thinking of the Chief Medicine Pipe called the Feathered Pipe. He decided to look for the tipi of the man who then owned the Pipe. When he found it, Bull Lodge began to cry at the tipi entrance, and after he had cried for some time, the medicine man spoke to him.

"Child," he said, "come inside." Bull Lodge went in and sat down. The medicine man asked, "What is it you want, and why are you crying at my tipi?" And Bull Lodge said, "I ask you to do me a favor. I ask you not to move the tribe away from this present site until I return. I am going to Black Butte, south of the Big River, to fast."

"I will stay here and wait for you," answered the medicine man. "The tribe will not move from this place until you come back." After leaving the tipi of the Feathered Pipe, Bull Lodge said to himself, "Now I will see if all this that has been revealed to me is to take place as it was told."

The First Vision

Bull Lodge walked out away from the camp, looking for a high hill not too far away. When he found one, he went to the top, took off his clothes and began to cry. He spent a long time crying on this hill, standing facing west. Finally the rain came. It was a brief shower, a heavy downpour which did not last long. It passed as suddenly as it came. He gathered up his clothing and put his robe over himself, carrying his soaked clothes home. Then he went to bed and slept peacefully.

At this time the tribe was camped near White River by a place called Cliffs, on the south side of the Big River (the Missouri) near

2. This butte stands alone on the eastern end of the Judith Mountains, near Lewistown, Montana.

the Belt Mountains.

Early the next morning , Bull Lodge called his friend Sits Like A Woman and asked him to accompany him to Black Butte, where he was told to fast. They went off together on horseback, and when they reached the butte, the sun was high in the sky. Bull Lodge told Sits Like a Woman to take his own horse back to camp with him. When he was alone at the foot of the butte, he took off his clothes. Then he started his ascent, taking only his robe, his knife and his pipe.

Before he reached the top of Black Butte, Bull Lodge could already feel the pangs of thirst. It was a hot, clear summer day. At the top, he began to cry. He cried for the rest of that day, resting only at short intervals. When evening came he built a small low shelter out of rocks, just big enough to lie in. The rock shelter was about two feet high and as long as he was tall. It was open at one end, in the shape of a "U". He gathered some evergreens and laid them inside as a mat to lie on. He lay down here whenever he rested, but every hour that he was awake, he cried.

Days and nights passed, and Bull Lodge became weaker and weaker. On the sixth day, just before the sun rose, he numbed the little finger of his left hand by hitting it, then he took out his knife and cut the finger off at the first joint below the nail. Taking the severed finger, he laid it on a rock and offered it up as a sacrifice. Shortly after this, he lay down. The loss of blood, coupled with his weakness from fasting, caused him to pass out.

Bull Lodge lay there all day and night, until the next morning after sunrise. During that time he had a vision. An old man appeared to him and said: "This first experience is a test to see if you are truly earnest in your ambition to become a great man of your people. The first test is the most severe, to find out your endurance and your will to become a great man. You have proven yourself worthy. Therefore all the things you desire will be given to you, but you are still obliged to go through the rest of the fasting. From time to time, these things I speak of to you shall be revealed at the designated place of fasting, a little each time. Because of what I now give you, this first of the fasting places shall be known as the place of the gift. At the second place, you will be instructed how to use what I shall give you here. My child, you must go back and live a quiet and respectable life. It will be revealed to you when and where you are to fast again.

35

"You are destined to complete your fasting on the seven designated buttes. At each one you will be told to go on. The length of time you will spend on each butte will be less and less, until you have finally completed your fasting on all seven. This first time, you were obliged to fast and pray for seven days and nights. The second will be shorter: you will fast and pray on another butte for six days and nights. On the third, you will remain five days and nights. On the fourth butte you will remain four days and nights; on the fifth, three days and nights; on the sixth, two days and nights; on the seventh and last butte you are sent to, you will stay but one day and night. This is all I will tell you for this time, my child. Now look to where the sun comes up."

Bull Lodge looked off, and there on the horizon he saw horses coming. One dark-colored horse ran ahead of the rest. The sun was just topping the horizon, shining on the lead horse's hide so that it looked glossy, like an otter skin. A tanned piece of hide hung around the lead horse's neck, with two buffalo hoofs strung on it like bells. Then Bull Lodge looked to the south of where he was and saw a tipi. It was painted several different colors and faced east to the sun's rising. The horse with the buffalo hoofs strung round its neck led all the horses up to the tipi entrance and stopped there. The whole herd was strung out on the horizon behind him, with the sun behind. And more horses kept appearing on the horizon, to swell the numbers of those at the tipi entrance.

Then the old man spoke again. "My child, I give you horses and a tipi. The first horse you own will be a smoky, buckskin-colored one. Then you will accumulate a herd. I give you that tipi and that herd of horses, my child. You shall do great things in healing and curing. You shall become a great doctor. Now you must go home and wait for the message to go to the next place of fasting. You have endured the most severe experience that was allotted to you, and your wishes are all granted."

When Bull Lodge woke from his sleep, the sun was already quite high. He knew that he had slept out the seventh day and night. He picked up his robe and pipe and started down to the bottom, where he had left his clothes eight days before.

In the meantime, the man who owned the Chief Medicine Pipe called the Feathered Pipe was concerned about Bull Lodge's absence. Bull Lodge said he would be gone a few days, but this was the morning of the eighth day and he still had not returned. The medicine man called Sits Like A Woman and asked him to go back to the place where he had left his friend. He was afraid Bull Lodge had met with some accident, or that a band of warriors from some other tribe had run into him on the butte and killed him. Black Butte was a well-known place for war parties going through. They all wanted to go up and look around.

So Sits Like A Woman set out to find his friend. When he reached the butte where he had left Bull Lodge eight days before, he looked up before climbing it and saw Bull Lodge slowly coming down. He was so weak, he was staggering as he came. When he reached the bottom where his clothes were, he could hardly put them on. Then Sits Like A Woman helped him onto the horse he had brought. They travelled home very slowly because of Bull Lodge's condition.

Thus Bull Lodge made a successful start toward his life's ambition. He set himself to the task of preparation by living a quiet and normal life. He was careful about his behavior. He practiced charity and showed respect for his elders and his tribe. At home, he spent most of his time pondering his experiences. He knew that he was to go through such experiences from time to time, and that they would be spaced at long intervals, but not evenly. Some would come sooner than others. So he bided his time patiently, waiting to be told what to do next.

The Second Vision

About a year after the first fasting experience, the Gros Ventre tribe was travelling north and had camped on the north side of the Big River, almost directly south of the western end of the Many Buttes (Bear Paw Mountains). One night in his sleep, Bull Lodge was told to go to the butte called Grows Tallest, now known as Old Baldy. He was to sleep on top of that butte for six days and nights.

The time to prepare for the second experience had come. Bull Lodge waited until late the next evening, then he went out into the hills and began to cry. After he had passed a considerable time crying, he saw a dark cloud coming from the west. In no time the cloud was over him. Lightning, hail and a downpour of rain came, but the storm passed as suddenly as it had come. (Remember Bull Lodge's instructions: before going out to fast on a particular butte by command, he was to go into the hills, where it would rain upon

him and purify him.) The next morning he sought out his friend
Sits Like A Woman and asked him to go with him to Grows Tallest
Butte where he was to fast. So they started for the Many Butte
Mountains, where Grows Tallest stands, and arrived at the top
early in the afternoon.

Before Sits Like A Woman left, Bull Lodge asked him to cut his
flesh so he could make a sacrifice. Sits Like A Woman cut three
strips of half circles on the lower part of Bull Lodge's chest. The
three strips were about an inch apart, rising one over the other
from the lower part of the chest to the center. The ends of each half
circle were about six inches straight across.

After Sits Like A Woman had finished cutting, he held the
strips of flesh up to the Supreme Being. Keeping his arm upraised,
he said, "Here is this flesh which is a sacrifice to you. The giver of
this flesh gives you his body. Look down on him and pity him and
grant him what he asks of you. Give him long life, wealth, and
power."

After uttering these words on his friend's behalf, Sits Like A
Woman placed the strips of flesh on a stone, then he left his friend
and went home. Alone, Bull Lodge began his crying. He cried all
the time he was not resting, sleeping or praying. He kept this up for
six days. On the sixth night when he lay down and fell asleep, a
small boy came to him in a dream. "My father wants you," he said.
Then Bull Lodge got up and followed the boy, who led him down the
east slope of the butte to a small cliff of rocks. The boy told Bull
Lodge it was a door, and that he was to enter. As Bull Lodge
entered, he saw that it was a tipi inside, and that the ground was
red, as if painted. He looked around and saw an old man seated at
the back of the tipi just to the right of center. Then the old man
spoke. "Your crying has aroused the pity of my son and my wife."
Bull Lodge looked around again. To his left, an old lady was sitting.
Her head was bowed and a robe was draped over her shoulder. He
saw half of a red-painted robe spread out on the ground at the back
of the tipi. The old man told Bull Lodge to sit on that robe. When
Bull Lodge had done so, the old man spoke again.

"It has been foretold that you would be here. You have been
destined to go through many difficult experiences. The hardship
was to be greatest at the beginning, and would gradually become
easier as you disposed of each trial, until you had undergone
everything. It will be just as it was told to you when you started.

This is your second experience. The hardship is not as severe as with the last one. The next will not be as hard as this. The time after will be shorter, and the next one after that will be still shorter. So it will be until all seven experiences are undergone. Now it was told to me by the one who attended your last experience, that I was to provide you with instruction concerning gifts that have already been given to you. Now, my child, look over there." The old man pointed east.

It was as though Bull Lodge were seeing a picture shown on a screen. He saw a large party of warriors riding in a northerly direction. Another war party was advancing upon the first from the north. Evidently a battle was going to take place. He looked again at the first group and saw a lone man advancing before it, carrying something on his back. The two parties began firing at each other. Bull Lodge saw the lone man transfer that object from his back to the front of his body. He was reaching with his right hand to his left and drawing the mysterious object before him, and as he did so, Bull Lodge recognized the man as himself. And the object was the shield that had been given to him when he was a boy of twelve, at the beginning of his spiritual life. Now a terrific battle was in progress before his eyes, and he himself was the star performer.

The lone man went up and down ahead of the line of his war party, always keeping his shield between himself and the enemy. Finally the enemy were routed. They fled, and the battle ended.

Then this man took his shield, gripping it at both sides where the thong attached, and held it out at arm's length before him. He shook it, as if shaking dirt off gently, and Bull Lodge could see bullets falling off the shield. As they fell they sounded like pebbles hitting the ground. Then the vision disappeared. And the old man said, "The battle which you have just witnessed shows part of what I am to teach you. You have seen for yourself how it was performed with the shield, that same shield which was given to you before. Even from this distance you noticed the double row of eagle feathers on its rim. It will always be recognizable as far as it can be seen. That will be the sign of its power."

"Now that you have been shown how to use the shield that was given to you, you will use it in all your battles and you'll become a great warrior chief. This is what I give you — chieftainship. You will be a leader in wars and you will never be wounded. You will be widely known among many tribes."

When the old man had finished telling Bull Lodge these things he said, "I will now instruct you regarding what was given to you to become a great doctor."

A small round hollowed shell and a small spoon made of buffalo horn were placed before Bull Lodge. The hollow shell had a little water in it, colored blue. The horn spoon also had a little water in it, colored red. Then the old man said, "This colored water is medicine made for blood flow. With this you can stop bleeding from a gunshot wound inside as well as outside of the body. You can stop a hemorrhage of any kind, anything where blood is flowing. The blue water is medicine to drink. It will cut through any kind of congestion of the human body, especially where one cannot discharge urine."

"No matter how severe these cases may be for which I am instructing you, you will not fail when you administer these medicines to a patient. First take a sip of it yourself. Then tell the patient to open his mouth. Then, as you pour a small amount of medicine into the patient's mouth, you will blow into the mouth. Blow while the medicine is poured, and the hemorrhage through the mouth will stop instantly. And with the blue medicine too, do the same thing to the patient, and the medicine will take action instantly."

Then the old man said to Bull Lodge, "Now that I have taught you a medicine which will make you famous in doctoring, you will have to drink these medicines yourself. Drink the red one first, then drink the blue one." So Bull Lodge swallowed the medicine. And the old man said, "I have done all that I was to do in the way of teaching you how to use the gifts that have already been given you."

Then the old man said to Bull Lodge, "Now it is my turn to give you some things myself. Outside as you leave you will see an animal, which I give you. But the animal himself must teach you about the power he will give."

"Now look around in my tipi," said the old man. And mysteriously, the tipi was filled with all the things that are found inside the tipi of a wealthy family. It was crowded with possessions. The old man told Bull Lodge, "In the future your tipi will look the way you see the inside of mine now. That is what I give you. You will be wealthy in property. The people of your tribe are keeping it for you." (He meant as a doctor, that he would be paid for his healing by his people.) Then the old man said, "My son, I have performed my responsibility to you as it was required of me. Now it will be up to the next one in turn to show you whatever he has in store for you. You can go home now, my son."

As Bull Lodge left the tipi, he saw a large grizzly bear standing upon its haunches a little way from the entrance. It stood there long enough for him to get a good look at it, then it disappeared. Then Bull Lodge woke up.

Looking around he saw the sun topping the Fur Cap Mountains to the east. So he picked up his robe and with the experience still fresh in his mind he went down the butte called Grows Tallest, descending to its bottom on the south side, the way he came up. There he waited for his friend Sits Like A Woman, and they went back to the Gros Ventre camp together. Now Bull Lodge wondered about the grizzly bear, and the meaning it held for him as it was foretold by the old man of the butte called Grows Tallest. Again he took up his normal life, just as when he had come home from his sleep on the first butte. But the thought of the grizzly bear never left his mind.

Bull Lodge bided his time patiently, all the while memorizing everything that had been told to him in the first and second experiences. He did not know where he was to fast next, and he kept expecting to be ordered there. Any time, as the tribe moved about, they might be near a butte where he would be ordered to go and sleep. So he waited, carefully meditating upon all that was revealed to him.

One night in his sleep he heard someone singing. He looked around and saw a man coming toward him. The man was singing as he walked, and he carried a branch in his hand. When he reached Bull Lodge he stopped and laid the branch down before him. "I bring this for you," he said. "This act is what was foretold to you about me in your last experience. This branch will be for your use in the future." Bull Lodge looked up from the branch. There was the grizzly bear he had seen on Grows Tallest, after he had finished his fast. Then the bear disappeared. (This meant that Bull Lodge was given the power to make berries whenever the need arose. The song was for Bull Lodge to sing before he performed the berry-making ceremony.)

41

The Third Vision

Now the tribe was up north in the vicinity of Three Buttes, which is now known as the Sweet Grass Hills, and they were heading back south. By the time they finally moved to the Little River (Milk River), it was early fall. As he slept here one night, Bull Lodge was told to fast on Last Butte in the Many Buttes, now called the Bear Paw Mountains.[3]

Bull Lodge was told to stay on this butte for five days and five nights. He asked his friend Sits Like A Woman to go with him and bring his horse back to camp. When they arrived, Bull Lodge again asked his friend to cut his flesh for sacrifice. Sits Like A Woman did this just as he did before, except the flesh was cut a different way. Instead of cutting strips, the arm flesh was stuck with an awl and the skin raised taut and cut off, making hole-like openings. This was done in four places about one inch apart. The row of holes down the outside of the right arm started just below the joint of the shoulder. The same was done to three places on the left arm, so that the total on both arms equalled seven. After Sits Like A Woman had finished cutting the flesh, praying with the pieces and dedicating the sacrifice, he left.

Now Bull Lodge began his customary devotions, crying and praying while going without food or drink. He did this for five days, sleeping when exhausted and concentrating when awake. On the fifth night his experience was telling on him, and he lay down and slept. In his dream a small boy approached him saying, "My father wants you, and I came to call you." Bull Lodge followed the boy, who took him down the east slope of the butte. Near the bottom, about two-thirds of the way down, the boy stopped at a door and opened it and told Bull Lodge to enter. Bull Lodge looked around inside and it was a tipi. An old man sat in the back to one side. He raised his head and looked at Bull Lodge. "My child, come and sit by me," he said, "I have been expecting you. I know all that has happened before this and everything that has been given to you. There's not much I can give because you already have been given

3. This butte is situated on the northeast end of the Bear Paw Mountains south of the town of Chinook, Montana, and is now called McCann Butte. It sits apart from the main range of mountains.

many things that are of great value to you and your people for the future. But at least I can give you something that will come in handy. Look, my son."

Bull Lodge looked where the old man was pointing, and there was the lake that lies at the foot of this butte on the south side. Coming out of the lake he saw a gray horse with a long flowing mane and tail. After it came horse after horse, until finally a large herd was gathered beside the lake. The gray horse was decorated with red paint, running from its forehead down its mane and back, along its full length and even down its tail. Around its neck was a narrow strip of tanned hide, also painted red. And two tips of a mountain goat's horns, about four to six inches long, hung like bells from this red strip of skin.

Then the old man said, "I give you the decoration on that horse. Look carefully at it. See how the horse is painted and what it has around its neck. You must do that to your horse whenever you go forth to battle on horseback. If you do that, your horse will never be wounded. The necklace on the horse is for fleetness. When you put that necklace on your horse it will be fast and show great endurance, especially in battle. And anytime you want your herd of horses to increase, paint your gray horse the way you see that one painted down there, only in addition paint its shoulder and hip joints red and turn it loose in the herd."

Then the old man told his wife, who was inside the tipi, to unfasten a bird that was tied to one of the poles to the right of where Bull Lodge sat. The old woman got up and untied the bird and brought it to her husband.

The old man showed it to Bull Lodge. "Take a good look at this bird. You know it because it is a common bird and is well known." (It was a woodpecker.) "Now my son, I give this bird to you. You will use it in the future and it will make you famous. You will be able to save a person even if he is sick and about to die. Now I have done my part by you, my son. It has been decided that you must complete the experiences, but as you finish each, the next will not be as severe as those before. You have gone through this experience successfully, my son. What you have already endured proves that you are sincere in your purpose. Now you can go home and bide your time, until you are ordered to the next place where you must sleep."

Bull Lodge awoke and looked around. Seeing that the sun was

about to rise, he gathered up his robe and started down the butte to await Sits Like A Woman.

At home he pondered over the bird that was given to him (the woodpecker) and he would think, "I wasn't told how to use this bird. I wonder what I must do about it. Perhaps later on someone will tell me how to use it."

The Fourth Vision

Bull Lodge took life very seriously now that he had these experiences. He had been shown many things, and he memorized them as he bided his time waiting for his next orders. He knew he had to go through four more experiences yet.

Meanwhile the tribe continued its customary wanderings from place to place, and a year later it was camped at Grows Tallest Creek (now known as Beaver Creek), which starts at the foot of Grows Tallest Butte in Many Buttes Mountains.[4] On the first night the tribe was camped at that creek, Bull Lodge was ordered in his sleep to go to the butte called Scraper[5] and fast.

Bull Lodge went out on the hills that evening, and the rain came just as he had been told it would before he went to fast. Early the next day he went out to Scraper Butte, going by himself this time. Upon reaching the place where he was to sleep, Bull Lodge began his customary acts of crying and praying. When tired he would lie down and rest, but throughout his waking time he continued to cry and pray. This was the fourth of the seven experiences he was to undergo, and since each was to be shorter than the last, he knew that he was to be here four days and four nights.

When he lay down and fell asleep on the fourth night, a small boy appeared to him and said, "My father wants you. I came to call you." Bull Lodge followed the little boy down the east slope of the same butte where he was fasting. Along the slope they came upon a tipi entrance. The little boy made him enter. Bull Lodge looked around inside and saw an old man and an old woman sitting there. "My son," said the old man as soon as Bull Lodge entered, "come and sit down over here by me." The old man was seated in the back

4. This creek starts on the north side of the butte and runs north, emptying into the Milk River above Havre, Montana.
5. Scraper Butte, now called Studhorse Butte, stands on the western end of Many Buttes, or the Bear Paw Mountains.

of the tipi. He moved to his left while speaking, making room for Bull Lodge on his right side. The old woman was then sitting to Bull Lodge's right, but not close.

Bull Lodge noticed a dish with water in it just behind the fireplace and in front of the old man. Bull Lodge wondered what that dish of water was for. The old man turned to Bull Lodge and said, "My son, move over a little ways." So Bull Lodge moved over, and after moving a ways he looked back to where he had moved from, and there he saw a man lying on his back. He had just appeared there mysteriously, and it seemed to Bull Lodge that the man was in pain. A black cloth covered the face and torso of the sick man. Then the old man said to Bull Lodge, "My son, you must watch everything I do very closely."

Then the tipi door opened and a group of men and women entered. There were seven men, and they lined themselves up on the old man's left hand side and sat down. And six women lined up on the opposite side and sat down to the right of the old woman. After they all were seated the old man took down his drum and laid it beside the dish of water. After making incense for his drum, he started to sing. He sang one song four times, then he sang a different song, also four times. This was only for Bull Lodge's benefit, so he could learn the two songs. Then the old man started to sing the first song again, and after singing it four times he handed the drum to the first man nearest him and told him to go ahead and sing.

Then the old man told Bull Lodge, "Watch closely, my son. What I am going to do is what is given to you, and I am to show you how." So Bull Lodge faced the old man and the sick person who was still lying on his back. In the old man's hand Bull Lodge saw a feather, which he immediately knew to be a woodpecker's tailfeather. The old man turned and held the feather over the incense smoke. Then he turned to the patient covered with the black cloth. When the old man raised the cloth, Bull Lodge saw a black mark on the man's belly. It was evidently put there with charcoal. It was about six or eight inches long, to one side of the navel. The singing of the seven men and six women continued, as it was for that purpose they were present.

Then the old man placed the point of the woodpecker's tailfeather upon one end of the black mark on the patient's belly. Holding the end of the feather where it is largest and smoothest, he mimicked the woodpecker. It was just the way the woodpecker sounded. As the old man made these sounds, the tailfeather entered into the patient's belly. The old man began to cut as if with a knife, and Bull Lodge heard the sound of cutting as if it really were a knife. When the feather reached the other end of the black line on the patient's belly, the old man took it out and laid it aside. Then he turned about and incensed both hands with smoke. Turning back, the old man put his right hand into the cut. Bull Lodge could see him feeling around for something inside the patient's body. When the old man took his hand out he had a round-looking object that just fit the palm. On this object Bull Lodge could see a dim mark, like the slit of a frog's mouth. The old man put it into the dish with water, which Bull Lodge had noticed when he entered. The singers stopped as soon as they saw the object laid in the dish.

The old man lit his pipe then and began to smoke. After puffing a few times he blew the smoke upon the cut in the patient's belly. He did this four times. Then the old man covered his patient with the black cloth and continued to smoke. After blowing on the black cloth with smoke four times, he laid the pipe down and raised the black cloth from the patient. Bull Lodge saw a small red scar where the belly was cut, but the cut was miraculously healed.

Next the old man attended to the object he had removed from the patient's body, which had been placed in the dish. He took the woodpecker feather and began cutting this object into slices. Then he fed a slice to each of the men and women who sang for him while he was operating. What was left of the slices he himself ate. After he had eaten it, the old man spoke to Bull Lodge. "My son, this is what you will do with the woodpecker feather that was given to you at the last butte you slept on." Then Bull Lodge spoke up. "My father," he said, "I will not take the part of this doctoring where you fed the slices of that object to the singers and ate some yourself. But I will accept the part where you did the cutting on the person's body."

"All right, my son," said the old man. "You are not forced to take what you do not want. You can go home, for your experience here is done. And my task is done, for it was assigned to me to show you how to use the bird that was given to you on the butte called Last Butte.

"My son, watch yourself carefully now that you are almost through with the experiences which have been allotted to you in your quest. You have the favor of those whose duty it is to watch over the children of the Supreme Being. Now go, my son, and wait until you are told to repeat your fasting at the next designated place."

Bull Lodge woke up and looked around. At a glance he saw that it was just about sunrise. So he gathered up his robe and started down the butte in the direction of the Gros Ventre camp that was then at Grows Tallest Creek.

The Fifth Vision

Bull Lodge returned to the customary life of his people. But in his leisure he would sit and ponder the events which had happened to him, memorizing them exactly in the order in which he experienced them, from beginning to end.

The Gros Ventre tribe continued its custom of moving from place to place. When winter set in it would find a place where wood and water was plentiful, and stay until early spring. They would begin moving to higher places when the early Chinook winds and the floods came, driving them from low ground. So it happened that the following year in the early summer, the tribe was camped at a lake called Bull Grunt. It is situated on the west side of the Many Buttes (Bear Paw) Mountains, northwest of the present site of Big Sandy, Montana. This lake, which is now called Lonesome Lake, is one of the habitual camping areas of the Gros Ventre tribe. On the first night Bull Lodge was told to go to Bear Paw Butte and sleep there.[6] So he went out that evening to let the rain cleanse him before his fast.

The next morning Bull Lodge left and took his nephew with him to bring his horse back to camp. When he was alone on Bear Paw Butte, he busied himself with erecting a shelter of rocks, of the same kind he had made in his first fasting experience. The rocks were piled up in a "U" shaped wall about two feet high for a windbreak. Evergreens were laid inside for a mat. This place on Bear Paw Butte was to be the fifth where Bull Lodge was to sleep. Since he had spent four days and nights on Scraper Butte, he knew Bear Paw Butte would require three days and nights of fasting.

6. This butte, now called Square Butte, is low with a flat top. It stands north of the western end of the Bear Paw Mountains, near the present town of Box Elder.

47

After making his shelter, Bull Lodge began his usual custom of crying and praying during all of his waking time. When he got tired he lay down in the shelter. He did this for three days and two nights. On the night of the third day as he lay dreaming, a small boy appeared to him. "My father wants you and I came to call you," he said. "Follow me and I'll show you the entrance to his tipi."

To Bull Lodge's surprise the boy led him in the opposite direction to that taken in the other fasts. The entrance to this place also surprised him, for it was on the bottom of the west side of the butte. When the little boy reached it, he told Bull Lodge to enter. Bull Lodge went in and found himself in a tipi. Looking around, he saw an old man sitting at the back. He immediately addressed Bull Lodge. "Come and sit down by me, my son. I have been expecting you, for it was known that you were to sleep here on my butte. I am to help you with your purpose of becoming a great man among your people.

"The time of accomplishing what is required of you is almost here. You have yet two places to fast before you are finished, and I am the fifth in turn to help you. I will give you medicines which will help you become a great doctor, including the power to take out of a person that which cannot be discharged by his system. I will give you five different kinds of medicines, and I'll also give you the power to make tobacco, matches, coffee, and sugar. The first medicine I will give you will be for consumption. The next will be for the fits. The third will be for childbirth, and the fourth for gun wounds. The last power will be for headaches. The roots for all the medicines which you will use will be found right near this butte."

Then the old man told Bull Lodge, "Now I will show you how to treat a person afflicted with consumption. My son, move over a little ways so you can see what I do. And watch me very closely as I perform." So Bull Lodge moved away and again there mysteriously appeared a person lying on his back, right behind the place where he and the old man had been sitting. This person was in pretty bad shape. It could be seen that he was in an advanced stage of consumption, even though he was covered with a black cloth from his head to just below the waist. The old man slowly made incense and incensed his hands. Then he blew his breath on the patient four times, one right after the other. The old man rubbed his hands on the ground gently. Taking a small pinch of charcoal between his thumb and forefinger, he ground it between them. From this he blackened his lips, both upper and lower.

The old man raised the black cloth from the sick man, and Bull Lodge saw the patient as if he were looking at an x-ray. He could see the lungs and stomach. The old man began to sing, and after singing the song four times he began drawing with his mouth on the patient's chest, as if he were sucking the skin. After drawing what might be considered a mouthful, the old man would spit it out into a hollow dish which he had placed beside himself. Bull Lodge looked at the stuff the old man spat into the hollow dish. It looked like pus and it was speckled with blood. The old man kept up this drawing process until he could not draw any more out, then he spoke to Bull Lodge. "Now this medicine which I will give you, you will boil in water and give to the patient to drink. You will doctor the patient just once as I have shown you. Then give him this medicine to drink. You will give him the medicine three times. That will make four times that you have treated the patient, and then he will be well." (Here Garter Snake Woman added that she saw her father treat a man named Spear in his later years and cure him of consumption.)

Then the old man said, "Now that I have shown you how to doctor for consumption, I will show you how you must be approached with a pipe when you are called to treat someone, and also what you are to do as you accept the pipe."

"The one who is assigned to call you doctor must, after entering your tipi, approach you by going to his left and addressing you on your right. The pipe must be held out before him with both hands, his right hand on the stem near where the stem and pipe connect, and his left hand on the pipe. When he reaches your position, the stem will be pointing to your left and the pipe will be between yourself and the man holding it. You then take the pipe with both hands on the stem, and he releases it. Holding the pipe before you in your left hand, run your right hand along the ground gently. Then stroke the full length of the pipe with your right hand, stroking from the pipe end along the stem towards yourself. Do this once with your right hand, then change the pipe from your left to your right hand and repeat this act with your left hand stroking the pipe and stem. You must do this twice with each hand, so that you stroke the pipe and stem four times. Then put the stem in your mouth and draw on it twice. Then light it and blow the smoke once above the pipe, holding it near your mouth. Then draw the smoke again and blow it above and below the pipe, still holding it near your mouth. Blow the smoke two times above the pipe and two times below and under the pipe. That will make it four times in all that you blow smoke.

"After that is done, pass the pipe to the man who first approached you with it, and he will smoke with you until the kinnickinnic is smoked up. Then he must go out by making a complete circle inside the tipi, continuing out the way he came in."

Bull Lodge said that at this time on Bear Paw Butte he was being tested. He felt some of this experience was a little foolish. (But Garter Snake Woman did not explain why Bull Lodge felt this way.)

Then the old man said to Bull Lodge, "Now these medicines which I am giving you are to be boiled in water before being given to the patient. When the medicine is ready, stand up near the patient and hold up the container with medicine and pray. After praying, extend your right hand with the container of medicine. As you do this, begin to sing. Now hold the container in your left hand and circle it around the patient, starting from his right side to his left. Go around the back to his left and on to his front, keeping the container about shoulder high to him. Then put the container in your right hand and circle it too, just like you did with your left hand. All this time you will be singing and the patient will be drinking the medicine from your hand. When the patient has finished drinking the medicine in the container, you will stop singing. Every time you do this and sing this song, I will hear you."

Then the old man told Bull Lodge, "Now that I have done my part for you, my son, you will go home.[7] You are about done with your experiences as they were allotted to you and you are proving yourself. You will be glad when it is all done and you have passed all the tests that must be accomplished. You will be known far and wide, and your people will depend upon you. But there are two other buttes that you will be sent to sleep on, so you must be patient and wait until you are told to go."

Then Bull Lodge woke up. Seeing that it was just about sunrise, he gathered his robe about himself and started down the

7. It was here, at Bear Paw Butte, that Bull Lodge was given the power to make tobacco, matches, coffee and sugar. But Garter Snake Woman did not tell how Bull Lodge made these four articles.

butte. When his nephew came, he took his horse and they rode back to the camp at the lake called Bull Grunt. Bull Lodge drifted back into the routine life of his people just as before, and set himself to memorizing the experiences of his fast on Bear Paw Butte.

The Sixth Vision

In its custom of moving from place to place, the tribe continued to wander over that country. A year after the time he fasted on Bear Paw Butte, the tribe was camped at a small creek near the Three Buttes. Here Bull Lodge was called again. He began with his usual procedure, going out the evening before he was to fast to be cleansed with rain. The next morning Bull Lodge called his friend Sits Like A Woman and asked him to go to the foot of the middle butte.[8] When they arrived he asked Sits Like A Woman to cut his flesh for sacrifice. Sits Like A Woman performed this ceremony by cutting two strips off both arms. Each of the four strips was started just below the shoulder joint and extended down the arm about four inches.

After Sits Like A Woman finished cutting Bull Lodge's flesh, he handed the cut strips to Bull Lodge and left. Then Bull Lodge started up the butte alone, carrying the pieces of his flesh in his hand. When he reached the top, he prayed with them, offering them up to the Supreme Being. Then he laid them on a flat stone and began his crying and praying.

About midnight of the first night, he lay down to rest. The nights are long at that time of year, and he lay wide awake until daylight came. Then he got up and stood facing east. Soon he saw the morning star coming over the horizon. He remained standing there until the sun had risen. Then he took the four pieces of flesh he had laid on the stone and held them up to the rising sun, praying for a long and prosperous life.

He replaced the pieces of flesh on the flat stone and resumed his crying, continuing this throughout the day. All of this time he never smoked. When night came he lay down and fell asleep. He hadn't been asleep very long when he began to dream. A small boy appeared to him and said, "My father wants you, and I have come to

---

8. This butte was later named Gold Butte, after a gold strike there. It lies in the Sweet Grass Hills below the Canadian border, northwest of Chester, Montana. (GHC)

call you. Follow me and I'll lead you to his tipi."

They had not gone very far down the eastern slope of the butte when the little boy stopped and turned to Bull Lodge. "I am going to give you some advice," he said. "When you enter my father's tipi you will see all kinds of animals and birds tied to each of the tipi poles. My father is going to ask you to take your choice, and you can pick any one you desire to have as a gift. Now my advice is that you pick the bird tied to the center tipi pole directly back from the entrance. Now that I have told you what to do, let us go on." But first Bull Lodge thanked the boy and gave him a small gift.

Now when Bull Lodge came to the entrance, he was surprised that it seemed high. Being powerless to do otherwise, he went in directly. He noticed that he was entering high up near the top of the tipi. Then he felt himself being lowered mysteriously. When he was on the ground inside the tipi, he saw an old man sitting at its back, and an old woman there too, who was his wife. The old man said, "You have finally come, my son, and I have been expecting you. For it was destined that in the experiences you were to undergo, you would reach me when it was my turn. It is known by all of us who are interested, that you are permitted to receive powers which will make you a great man among your people. Come and sit before me, and face me."

Bull Lodge did this, and when he was seated the old man made incense. He held both of his hands over the incense with palms down, then he raised them over Bull Lodge's head and without touching him, drew his hands down along Bull Lodge's sides to the ground. The old man repeated this ceremony four times. Then he told Bull Lodge, "My son, look around in my tipi and see all the things tied to the tipi poles. Choose any one of them you desire, and I will give it to you."

Bull Lodge looked everything over, seeing every kind of bird and small animal there. Now since he had already been informed by the boy what he must choose, he just pretended to look the things over. When he thought he had taken enough time to make it appear he was uncertain, he looked at the bird the little boy told him to choose. He pointed to it and said, "My father, I'll take that bird tied to the center tipi pole at the back of the tipi." The old man bowed his head and spoke to his wife. "All right," he told her, "you can go ahead and give him what you are to give him."

The old woman got up and untied something from a tipi pole. It was the skin of a wolverine that was made into a bag. It was laced down its throat and chest. She approached Bull Lodge with the wolverine skin bag and stopped near him. She told him to turn around, face the front of the tipi and sit with his legs straight before him. He quickly obeyed. Then the old woman stood at his right, holding the skin bag firmly in both hands, her left hand on the neck part and her right hand on the hips of the wolverine skin bag. Raising it, she stroked Bull Lodge down his right side, drawing the skin bag down, until it touched the ground with the wolverine head forward. She then circled around him, stopping to stroke him down his left side. She repeated this act, stroking his right side and then circling around his back again and stopping once more behind him, where she stroked his left side again. Thus she circled Bull Lodge two times in all, stroking him two times on each side. She held her right hand on his head, gently resting it there, then took it away and put her left hand on his head. Then, very gently, she shook the wolverine skin bag.

"My son, I have pity on you," she told Bull Lodge. "I am a woman and usually it's hard for anyone to arouse my pity. There have been many men who have slept on my tipi (meaning the butte), but never before have I been moved to pity by them. This one time I am moved, that is why I am telling you now what I will do out of pity for you.

"Now my son, when I circled you, it signified that people all around you will be your children." (She meant that in taking care of their health, people would put him in the position of a father to his children.)

The old woman put the skin bag down. Going over to one of the tipi poles, she untied something from the pole — a small drum about twelve inches in diameter with a four-inch rim. She laid the drum down so that its surface faced up. Then she unloaded the wolverine skin bag, which was bulging. She began taking small bags out of it, laying them in a row across the surface of the drum until she had laid seven small bags down in a line running north and south. Then she said to Bull Lodge, "Now my son, look out there." She pointed outside. "See those plants there? Take a good look at them so you'll be able to recognize them when you see them again. Their roots are to be used by you for medicines to cure the sick."

"You have already been told what each medicine is for, and

these particular roots you are to use grow between two points—Three Buttes and the Bear Paw Mountains to the south. These plants only grow strung along between here and Bear Paw Butte." Then the old woman said, "My son, this is what I am doing for you. I am giving you additional power to cure, in return for what you gave my little son when you were with him outside of my tipi. It's the first time my little boy was given a present. Through that act of yours my pity for you was drawn out. That is all, my son."

Then the old man spoke. "My son, you were brought in through the top of my tipi, mysteriously. It was for a special reason. But now I'll take you out through the regular entrance." The old man began to sing, and as he did he began to move toward the east, where the entrance was. He sang the song four times, stopping for very short intervals before moving on again. The last time he stopped was at the entrance, outside, when his song had ended. Bull Lodge joined him there and the old man said, "My son, look yonder and observe closely what you see."

Bull Lodge looked out to where the old man pointed, and he saw a large company of people, decked out in weapons like a war party. As Bull Lodge watched, one man stepped out in the lead. He was carrying something on his back, something on his shoulders. This man stopped and took what he was carrying off his back, placing it on the left side. Then he faced east, to where the sun rises, and held up an object which Bull Lodge recognized as a shield. Putting both hands in front of him, he swayed the shield to the left and to the right four times, then he put it back on himself. Then another war party appeared, charging on this first group. But the first war party was ready, and the man with the shield immediately placed himself between the advancing warriors and his own people. Taking off the shield, he advanced on the charging warriors, holding the shield before him, and he began to sway it back and forth, left to right. He was wearing a white buffalo robe fastened under his chin, and the robe hung down to cover his entire body. The battle moved the two groups back and forth. First one party would advance, then the other. But this man's party was not losing any warriors, and they were killing many of the opposing party. The battle was brief. The enemy was defeated and fled.

When the battle was over, the man who had acted as the protector of his war party took off his white robe. He spread it out before him and shook it. Bull Lodge could hear something like small pebbles falling from the robe onto the ground, as the man shook it out gently. Then the old man spoke to Bull Lodge. "My son, that man you see out there with the shield is yourself. The shield you see is the shield that was given to you at the beginning of the experiences you have undergone."

"You were required to fast on this butte for two days and two nights. And just as it was told to you, each time you completed an experience, the next in turn would be shorter. What you have just seen out there of the battle, and of the man with the shield who wore the white buffalo robe, shows that when you are engaged in battle with your enemy, you will never be wounded. The shield and the robe will protect you from bullets. Also, your horse will never be wounded or shot down under you.

"This is your sixth experience, and you still have one more to finish. Then this part of your life will be accomplished. The first experience you went through, fasting for seven days and seven nights on Black Butte, was intended to test you. That decided whether you were sincere in your ambition to become a great man. If you failed through discouragement or lack of will power, it was intended that your efforts would go unheeded. The things that you have been receiving would pass away. But when you proved that you were sincere by passing the first test, it was decided that it would take a long time to give you all you wished and asked for. So it was that it had to be done according to our rule of seven times. Your life would be governed accordingly until you had completed all of the seven fasts, in order to receive all you asked for.

"Now my son, the next experience is the seventh and last you are to go through. You are to sleep on the westernmost of these buttes, and you are required to stay there for just one day and one night. You will not be taken inside as was done heretofore, but your entire experience will take place on top of the butte. Now you must go home and wait until you are ordered to go to the place which I have just told you about. The time will not be long before you will be told to go to that place."

Then Bull Lodge woke up and saw that it was just about sunrise. He gathered up his robe and started down the butte in the direction of the encampment, which he could see off in the distance, south of Three Buttes. He had gone to the buttes on foot and he returned to camp the same way.

The Seventh Vision

The tribe in its wanderings camped at that same creek late that summer and Bull Lodge was told in his sleep to go to a butte called Porcupine, on the west side of Three Buttes, the place of his last experience.[9] As usual, Bull Lodge went out the evening before he was to start, to receive cleansing from the rain. The following morning, very early, he woke his brother, whose name was Bear Goes on Side Hill. They went to the butte on horseback, tied their horses at the foot and started up. When they reached the top the sun was just appearing over the eastern horizon. Bear Goes on Side Hill cut his brother's flesh on both thighs. Four small, round pieces of flesh were cut on the right thigh in a vertical line, and three pieces were cut on the left thigh the same way, so that the number of pieces cut would be seven. Then his brother left. Bull Lodge took the pieces of flesh and held them up as a sacrifice to the Supreme Being, praying with them in his hand. Then he laid them on a flat stone and began his crying, which was his usual way of worshipping.

He did this all through that day and into the night. When he was tired he lay down and slept. He began to dream. An old man appeared to him, saying, "My son, I have been expecting you, for I was told of your coming to my place at this butte. I am the last one of the seven who are to help you become famous among your people. You have already got all you asked for and wanted, and have proven yourself worthy of our help. I have just one thing to give you. Come over here, my son."

Bull Lodge followed him, and a short distance from where the old man appeared, they came to a spot that was cleared of grass and smoothed clean. Then the old man said, "Look, my son. There are all the things that have been given to you." Bull Lodge looked over the cleared ground and saw all the things that had been given to him in his experiences. They were painted with red earth. Off to one side lay a whistle. The old man picked it up. "Here is what I am giving you. I will show you how you must use it when the occasion

9. This small butte stands about a mile west of Three Buttes, in the Sweet Grass Hills next to Alberta. (GHC)

56

arrives."

Suddenly a man appeared there on the cleared ground. He lay on his back with a bullet hole in his chest. Bull Lodge could tell he was dying, because his breathing came in gasps and far apart.

Standing at the head of the dying man, the old man blew the whistle four times, long and straight. Then he circled to the man's right, stopping at the feet, and blew the whistle four times, exactly as before, four times long and straight. Then he circled again, moving to his left, until he stood again at the head. Once more he blew the whistle, four times long and straight. Again circling to the left, the old man stopped at the dying man's feet. This time the old man blew the whistle four times spasmodically. Bull Lodge noticed that when the old man blew the whistle the third time, there was a change in the wounded man's breathing. It was almost normal. When the old man blew the whistle the fourth and last time, spasmodically, the patient opened his eyes and sat up, looking around.

The old man then turned to Bull Lodge and said, "Now my son, with this whistle I am giving you, you will be able to do just what you saw me do, no matter how near death a person may be. You will be able to restore life and cure him. Any time you do this with this whistle, you shall not fail, because when you blow on the whistle I'll hear it.

"My son, you have now finished with the experiences that were allotted to you. You have made it clear to us that you are sincere in your ambition to become a great man. All of the important things which go to help one become famous have been given to you. Now that your wish is granted and your work done, you are to wait until you are told to begin exercising the powers that are given to you. Go now and prepare yourself, my son. As it was told you, you must get ready for the life you are to live."

Then Bull Lodge woke up. Rising to his feet he prayed long and earnestly to the giver of all things. He thanked him for all that was revealed to him and for the many gifts, but especially for the supernatural powers attached to each one.

Bull Lodge was twenty-three years old when this experience of fasting was completed. He started at the beginning of his seventeenth year, and completed the course at the end of his twenty-third year.

At his leisure he began to gather material to make the articles that were given to him throughout the course of his experiences.

First he set out to make the shield, because it was the first article that was revealed and given to him. Then he made the others one by one in sequence, exactly as they were revealed to him.[10]

10. The following note provides useful information about the supernatural gifts described here by Garter Snake. It was forwarded by Mr. Richard A. Pohrt, drawing upon his acquaintance with tribal members contemporary with Garter Snake and his extensive knowledge of Plains Indian material culture. "The woodpecker given to Bull Lodge in his third vision (p. 43) is the red shafted flicker *(colaptes cafer collaris)* whose feathers appear in both Bull Lodge's war medicine bundle and his horse stealing bundle. His son, Curly Head, acquired the power to use the tailfeathers from his father. Three tribal members — Aloysius Chandler, The Boy and Thomas Main — told me they personally observed Curly Head perform surgical operations with it. They all remembered his way of honing the tailfeather by stropping it across the surface of water in a saucer, then testing it with his finger like a knife. Bull Lodge's war medicine bundle, which I acquired from Philip Powder Face in 1937, not only includes feathers of the red shafted flicker, but also the stuffed skin of a parrot and the stuffed and decorated skin of a western red squirrel *(sciurus hudsonicus richardsoni)*. I believe this is the bird and animal referred to in the second section of this narrative, on pages 64 to 66. The mysterious parrot was identified at the University of Michigan as *Ara macao,* whose range extends from Oaxaca, Mexico south to Bolivia. The bird and animal are shown on page 215 of *The Gros Ventres of Montana,* Part One, by Regina Flannery. I should add that the sweet pine needles Bull Lodge used for making incense are from the tree commonly known as Alpine pine but classified as Alpine fir or *Abies lasiocarpa.*" (GHC)

2. FROM WARRIOR TO HEALER

I. Bull Lodge's War Parties

This part of Bull Lodge's life history shows how he began to fulfill the purposes of the gifts given to him on the seven buttes. First came his war experiences. Keep in mind that I can only speak here of those which were supernaturally directed.[1]

The First War Party

The Gros Ventres were camped on the north side of the Big River at a place called Many Mounds of Rock, just below old Fort Benton. One night Bull Lodge was advised in a dream that his war experiences were to begin. He was to go south with sixteen men in his war party. In this dream he was told, "I give you horses and one man." Bull Lodge sought out Sits Like A Woman and described the

---

1. In this second part of Bull Lodge's story, Garter Snake Woman did not intend to represent the extent of his war experiences. She was telling only what her father included and Bull Lodge only told about that part of his life which was connected with the supernatural. Also, the part of his life which was not controlled by the supernatural was common knowledge and performed publicly. He spent ten years of his life as a warrior. During that time he used the special powers at his command to bring him to his desired goal of being a war chief.

dream. He asked his friend to go on this war party with himself as leader. They found fifteen trusted men and headed south. Now the land south of Elk River, now called the Yellowstone (in the area of Big Mountain Sheep River, Little Mountain Sheep River and Tongue River), was Crow country. And at this time the Crow people were bitter enemies of the Gros Ventre.

On the first night out, Bull Lodge left his party to go off a short distance. He cried and prayed far into the night before returning to camp for sleep. The next day they travelled steadily south and crossed the Shell River. They went on to Elk River, just above the place where Tongue River empties into it from the south, and stopped there. Bull Lodge sent Sits Like A Woman out as a scout. He returned after sighting a Crow camp on the south side of Elk River.

The war party waited until dark before going down along the river. They stopped directly opposite the camp and Bull Lodge selected four men in addition to Sits Like A Woman to go with him. They crossed the river and were fortunate enough to steal a large herd of horses. Then they crossed back and rejoined the main party. Bull Lodge went off by himself after everyone was safely hidden. He made medicine and sang a special song four times. He prayed to his Father, Mountain Man, to give him a human body. (By this he meant that he wanted a scalp.) When he finished praying, he blew his whistle four times.

He rejoined his party and after waiting a while, they heard singing just a short distance below where they were hidden. From the sound they knew the singers were headed for the river. Then Bull Lodge, Sits Like A Woman and two others set out to reach the river ahead of the singers. There were three Crow men, and they had brought pack horses along with those they were riding. The Gros Ventres ambushed them, killing all three of the Crows. Bull Lodge scalped one and took his black horse. The other two were also scalped and their horses and packs taken. Bull Lodge's party started for home immediately, travelling north for two days without stopping. When they reached Shell River they rested. Bull Lodge told his men that they would now be safe from pursuers, and that they should look for a buffalo for food.

The next day they reached Black Butte, which lies just east of the present site of Lewistown. This is where Bull Lodge had fasted for seven days and nights at the beginning of his spiritual experiences. Bull Lodge ordered his war party to halt at the foot of the butte and wait for him. He must go to the top, he said, to return to his Father something of what he had been given on the expedition. He caught the black horse and strung its owner's scalp around the neck. He rode it to the top of the butte, dismounted and prayed. "My Father, Mountain Man, see how I have brought these gifts. I offer them to you in thanks for the manhood you have given me. Here is the scalp of the man you gave me and the horse he owned." He shot the horse and left it there, descending on foot to rejoin his party.

They started north for the Big River in the late afternoon and camped for the night at Wolf Creek. The next day they reached the Big River directly south of Many Buttes Mountains. Crossing over to the north side they followed the river to a place known as Many Mounds of Rocks, which was where they had started south to invade the Crow country.

This was the first of the war experiences which were controlled supernaturally. Bull Lodge had completed his fasting experiences seven years before this war party. When he returned he resumed his usual life, biding his time until he would be ordered out again in the same way. He was now thirty years old.

The Second War Party

Early the following summer the tribe was camped on Belt River, near the Little Belt Mountains on the south side of the Big River. One night Bull Lodge was told in a dream to go south on the warpath and to take sixteen men with him, just as before. Bull Lodge again called on his friend Sits Like A Woman and they gathered fifteen trusted warriors. The next morning they started out for Crow country, which lay southeast of the Gros Ventre camp, and in a few days they reached the south bank of Elk River, just above the place where Big Mountain Sheep River empties into it.

Once again Bull Lodge sent his friend Sits Like A Woman out to scout. He reported that a number of Crows had camped below the mouth of Big Mountain Sheep River. That night Bull Lodge took Sits Like A Woman and two others to the south side of Elk River. They raided the Crow horses and drove them back across the river to their own camp. Then Bull Lodge told his war party, "We will wait here for those whom we are to get, those who were given to me. They are still to come."

The warriors waited on the north bank of Elk River. Soon four

Crows appeared, nearing the bank just a short distance below where they were hidden. They were travelling with a band of horses. Just as the Crows were preparing a raft to cross the river, Bull Lodge and his party charged them. Two were killed and two got away. Bull Lodge ordered his men not to pursue them. "We got two of them and their horses," he said. He scalped one of the men they had killed. When they rounded up the Crows' horses, they discovered that they had originally belonged to the Gros Ventres. Evidently the Crows had recently raided one of the Gros Ventre clans.

Bull Lodge's war party started north for home immediately, travelling quickly and steadily toward the Big River opposite Many Buttes Mountains. A small creek called Warm Spring empties into the Big River from the south at this place, where a trading post run by a white man was then located. (This trader was named Foot Cut Off by the Gros Ventre because he had no toes.) Bull Lodge and his warriors arrived early in the evening but they did not stop until they crossed the Big River. They camped for the night on the north bank.

The next day early in the afternoon they came to Many Buttes Mountains. They crossed the divide near Grows Tallest Butte and stopped for the night at the head of Grows Tallest Creek, where Bull Lodge had a special purpose for stopping. Late that evening he roped the Crow's buckskin horse and tied it up for the night, ready for him. Before daybreak he took it up to the top of Grows Tallest Butte, where he had fasted six days and nights. He tied the Crow scalp he had taken at Elk River around the horse's neck. The sun was rising as he rode onto the top of the butte. He dismounted and presented his gifts to his Father. "My Father, Mountain Man, here is the scalp and the horse I captured from the enemy for you. I give you these in return for what you have done for me. You have given me a good life, chieftainship and wealth." After saying this he shot and killed the horse and left it there as a sacrifice. Then he went down to the foot of the butte, where his party was waiting. They gathered the horses together and headed home.

The tribe had moved while Bull Lodge was away, and the returning war party was fortunate to find the camp as soon as they did. The new camp was on the Little River, above Havre at a place called White Hill. A human statue now stands on the spot. Thus Bull Lodge completed his second supernaturally directed war experience. Again he took up his normal life and waited for the moment when he would be told what he must do.

The Third War Party

About a year later the tribe was camped at Big Springs, where Lewistown now stands. Here Bull Lodge was again told in a dream to go on a war party. Again he asked Sits Like A Woman to accompany him, and they gathered the same number of warriors together. They rode to the south bank of the Big River and followed it until they reached the mouth of Elk River. Bull Lodge sent Sits Like A Woman out to scout for them. When he returned, he announced that he had sighted a Crow camp on the same side of the river, just below the mouth of Elk River.

When night came, Bull Lodge, Sits Like A Woman and two others crossed Elk River and stole into the Crow camp. They raided a herd of horses and drove them back to where the others were waiting. Bull Lodge and his smaller group immediately went back to the Crow camp. Just before they reached it, a man and a woman were seen coming toward them, then they turned off. Bull Lodge's party followed them, wishing to be far enough away from the Crow camp that a commotion would not be heard. The man and woman went to some horses that were tied up. The man untied the horses and started back towards the camp. Then he came back and put a saddle on one of the horses. Then the two of them rode down along the river bank. Bull Lodge's party circled ahead of them and attacked, killing the man and capturing the woman. Bull Lodge scalped the dead Crow warrior but ordered that the woman be turned loose. Then they rejoined the main body of the war party, taking the Crow's gray horse with them. It belonged to Bull Lodge now, because he was the leader of the smaller party.

They crossed to the west side of Elk River and started up the Big River on the south side until they came to the place where the Big Coullee (Cow Creek) empties into it. Crossing there they rode north to the Many Buttes Mountains, now called the Bear Paw Mountains. Bull Lodge ordered a halt there and they gladly rested, having ridden for two days and nights without stopping except to eat and blow the horses. Then from the Many Buttes they headed straight north to the Little River, or Milk River. Following it up to a place called Snake Weeds, which lies above the present location of Havre, they found the Gros Ventre camp.

The next day Bull Lodge and his nephew rode to Three Buttes, in the Sweet Grass Hills. They took the gray horse and Crow scalp with them. When they reached the foot of the middle butte, Bull Lodge told his nephew to wait. He strung the scalp around the neck of the gray horse and rode it halfway to the top of the butte. He dismounted at the very place where the old man had brought him out of the butte when he was fasting two days for his sixth vision. "My Father, Mountain Man," he prayed, "here is a scalp and a horse I captured. I give them to you." Then he shot and killed the horse and went back down on foot to meet his nephew. They did not reach camp until late that night.

Now during all of these war parties Bull Lodge carried the shield given to him when he began his fasting experiences, at the age of seventeen.

The Bird and the Ferret

One day Sits Like A Woman came to Bull Lodge in criticism. "My friend," he said, "were you really supposed to kill the horses you captured? Was it demanded of you to take them to those places and sacrifice them? I have been worried about this custom of yours, and I think you ought to quit doing it. It doesn't look right, that you kill the horses as you do." Bull Lodge thought about it a while, then he replied, "All right, I won't do it anymore."[2]

That night Bull Lodge had a vision in his sleep. A Man appeared before him holding two gifts in his hands. The Man wore a tanned buffalo hide for a robe, fastened under his chin. The entire robe was painted with the sacred red paint commonly used by Indians. He spoke to Bull Lodge, saying, "My son, I have come to bring you these things, in return for the horses and scalp you brought my little boy in the middle of Three Buttes. He was well

2. Bull Lodge shot captured horses at three different buttes where he had fasted: first at Black Butte, east of Lewistown, then at Grows Tallest Butte in the Bear Paw Mountains, and finally at the Middle Butte of the Sweet Grass Hills. The killing of the horses and the scalps tied around their necks are sacrifices to those who had appeared to him on these particular buttes, or as Bull Lodge put it, to Those Who Watched Over Him From Above. If these spiritual powers had continued to control his war experiences by commanding him to go out again, he would have done so and made sacrifices on other buttes where he had fasted. But since he was commanded to lead war parties only three times, he made a sacrifice on those three buttes only.

pleased. I give you these things to keep for your children, so that your sons will be noted chieftains, and your daughters recognized as leaders."

After saying these things, the Man laid a bird and a ferret in Bull Lodge's arms, so that both heads rested in his left arm. When Bull Lodge had received these gifts, the Man spoke again. "Now that you have done what was demanded of you concerning the war parties, there will be no more orders of that nature. You are to live normally, concentrating on a life that is true to the special powers given you, and on their proper use. Now, my son, I must leave you. Remember that from now on you must use your own judgment to guide yourself as a warrior. Once again you have proven yourself satisfactory to those who watch over you." The Man then disappeared, just as suddenly as he had appeared.

The next morning, as soon as Bull Lodge woke up he began rummaging around in the bedding. In doing so he aroused his wife's curiosity. She asked him what he was looking for, but he was not ready to tell her of his vision, so he didn't answer. Bull Lodge had married just before his last war party, and he was cautious about letting his wife know about his experiences. Now there had been a good thunderstorm that night. His wife had gotten up before it struck to erect a temporary inside shelter[3] over their bed. She left it up until after breakfast.

Bull Lodge was sitting on the opposite side of the bed, while his wife was unfastening the sheet to dry it out in the sun. She had taken it off the overhead rope and was unfastening the bottom when she suddenly cried out in alarm. "Come and see what these things are!" she called to Bull Lodge. But he immediately knew what they were and laughed at her fear. He got up and went over to look. They lay between the interior sheet and the tipi proper. "A, ho, a, ho!" he exclaimed, "I am glad of what is given to me. A, ho! my Father, how glad I am that you give me a living!" He picked up the bird and ferret, recognizing them as what the Man gave in his vision. Making a closer inspection of the gifts, he identified the

3. In the early days, the Gros Ventre way of keeping water from dripping on the bed was to string a rope across the tipi high overhead and parallel to the bed. A sheet was tied between this rope and the bottom of the tipi poles directly behind the bed. The stretched sheet made a steep slope over the bed for good drainage. The Sioux called this inside rain cover an *ozan*.

ferret immediately, but the bird was unknown to him. He had never seen it before or heard of it. It resembled a curlew and was about its size, but its bill was like that of a common prairie chicken. Its feathers were thickly dotted with every known color. The bird was impossible to identify. After examining the two gifts, Bull Lodge wrapped them and placed them where his shield customarily hung in the tipi.

After this Bull Lodge never led another war party. He was thirty-three years old when he performed the last of his supernaturally controlled war experiences. For seven years, however, until he was forty years old, he continued to be a noted warrior and was recognized as a superior fighter. The powers given to him in his visions were always at his command and he feared no one. He collected many scalps and trophies, and often raided enemies' herds of horses. Because of his outstanding record as a warrior, he was recognized as a war chief when he reached forty.

He had fulfilled his role as a warrior, and was considering becoming a medicine man. He began studying for this. He gathered together all the plants and roots that were given in his fasting experiences. He also made the doctoring implements that were given to him in visions.

II. The Healing of Yellow Man

Bull Lodge was now forty years old, and according to Gros Ventre tradition he was quite young to be a doctor. But because of the hardships he had endured since his youth, he was considered an exception. His constant practice of fasting and the deeds he accomplished publicly convinced the tribe of his sincerity in becoming a great man. At this time his compassion was aroused by the serious illness of his uncle, Yellow Man. Every day, Yellow Man's condition became worse. He was failing fast and getting weaker. When his uncle reached the stage where he had to be helped even to turn over in bed, Bull Lodge could not contain himself any longer, and he declared himself as a doctor.

He spoke to his mother, Good Kill. "I will consult my Father Above Man and tell him that my relative needs my help. I will doctor my uncle. Go and tell his father-in-law of my intention. Also tell him that I must be approached with a pipe filled with kinnic-kinnic, as is customary when a doctor is being called for his services. And tell him that not less than seven articles are to be given to me for my services."

The First Day

When Yellow Man's father-in-law heard this from Bull Lodge's mother, he was overjoyed, because he had observed the seven years of fasting and hardships Bull Lodge had undertaken. Yellow Man's father-in-law immediately made preparations for the calling of Bull Lodge to doctor the sick man. He ordered his son to catch seven head of their best horses and tie them up by their tipi, so that Bull Lodge could take them when he had finished treating Yellow Man.

Yellow Man's father-in-law filled a pipe with kinnickinnic and went to Bull Lodge's tipi. Standing where he entered, he asked Bull Lodge, "How must I approach you with this pipe? I have come to call you to doctor my son-in-law, your uncle Yellow Man." "Come to me from your left," said Bull Lodge, "and hold the pipe before you with stem foremost and with both your hands holding the pipe."

The man did that. Holding the filled pipe before him he came forward to the left and stopped before Bull Lodge, sitting on his bed at the back of the tipi. Bull Lodge took the filled pipe with both hands. Holding it in his left hand, he rubbed his right hand on the ground. He then stroked the whole pipe, starting at the far end and stroking towards his person. Then he changed the pipe to his right hand, and after rubbing his left hand on the ground, he stroked the pipe and stem toward himself. He performed this once more with each hand, so that the act was done four times.

He lit the pipe and smoked. The pipe was handed back and forth between Bull Lodge and the man who brought it, until the kinnickinnic was smoked up. Bull Lodge emptied the ashes of the pipe bowl by scraping it with a pointed stick, holding the pipe above his head for an instant, then bringing it down in front of him in his left hand. He emptied more of the ashes before passing the pipe to his right hand. Holding the pipe up as before, he emptied part of the ashes again, then he passed the pipe back to his left hand and repeated the procedure. Passing the pipe once more to his right hand, he emptied out all of the ashes. Thus he performed this act four times. He handed the pipe to the man and told him to go on past him, completing a circle in the tipi as he went out.

Yellow Man's father-in-law was told to call seven men and six women to sing Bull Lodge's medicine songs as he doctored. The seven men must take a place in the tipi to their right as they enter, and the six women must stand directly opposite to the seven men, going to their left as they enter. The patient must lie with his head toward the east, where the sun rises. A filled pipe with kinnickinnic is to be placed by his bed, with the stem pointing in the same direction. When this was done Bull Lodge was told the patient was ready.

Bull Lodge took his drum, his medicines, and the black cloth that he intended to use in his doctoring. Entering the tipi where the sick man was, he approached at the patient's left side. He sat down on the ground at the foot of the bed and took up his drum. Speaking to the men and women who were there to sing for him, he said, "I will sing my song three times. Then I will turn the drumming and singing over to you."

There was a man present named Many Tipis who was noted for his singing and quick memory. When Bull Lodge gave his song the third time, Many Tipis was singing it along with him. Many Tipis sang it himself the fourth time. Bull Lodge told the people that almost everything was done as it was supposed to be in the preparing of the tipi and patient. But one mistake was made. In the articles to be given to Bull Lodge for his services, he had told them he was commanded not to receive any weapons or anything that was sharp. This rule applied to the first four times that he doctored. But after the fourth time, he could receive weapons. Now Yellow Man's brother-in-law had given a gun, an arrow scabbard made of mountain lion's skin, an elk horn bow, and a robe with porcupine quill work in it, as well as seven horses. So the gun, scabbard and bow had to be replaced by two robes, to make it a proper gift for Bull Lodge at this time.

Bull Lodge stripped off his clothes, all but his breech cloth. Taking the red paint that is commonly used by the Gros Ventres, he painted all the scars on his arms, legs, and chest which had been made during his fasting experiences. He also painted his forehead and wrists. Then, taking the drum, he sang his song keeping time. He sang it four times, then he turned the drum and the singing over to the men and women who had come to sing as he doctored.

Bull Lodge placed a wooden bowl beside the patient. It was

about six inches in diameter from rim to rim and about two or three inches deep at the center of the hollow. A rainbow design was painted around the edge of the rim. The inside was all black, and the outside was dark red. Bull Lodge had made this wooden bowl out of a Box Elder burl, especially for doctoring purposes.

Yellow Man had been covered with the black cloth, and Bull Lodge removed it. Then he began to draw or suck with his mouth on the patient's chest. After each time Bull Lodge drew, he would spit the stuff into the wooden bowl. After doing this four times, he had the patient turned over, back up. Then Bull Lodge drew on the patient's back with his mouth. Again he did this four times, then the singing stopped. The stuff he had drawn out of the patient's chest and back was a mixture of yellow, green and brownish-colored matter.

Then Bull Lodge lit the filled pipe that had been laid beside the patient before he entered. After he had finished smoking, he took the black cloth that had covered the patient and stroked him with it. He drew it from the patient's head along his full length and shook it gently. He performed this four times.

Bull Lodge took his drum and sang his song four times over the patient. Before turning the drumming and singing over to the seven men and six women, he again doctored the patient by drawing on the chest and back with his mouth. He told those who were there that if his uncle were really bad off, he would doctor him seven times, but that if he were not so bad off, he would cure him by doctoring him four times. Bull Lodge ordered the singers to start up again while he covered the patient with a black cloth. He lighted the filled pipe and began smoking. Occasionally he would blow smoke on the cloth covering the patient. He did this four times. Then the singers stopped.

Then Bull Lodge gathered up the black cloth with both hands and stood up, raising the cloth and praying. "Father Above Man, I am grateful for these powers to heal and cure. Look down on me. I will raise a body up again." Turning east he repeated this, adding the words, "I am using the painting on the shield that you gave me." He turned to the south and repeated the prayer. He turned west and spoke the same prayer again. Then lowering the black cloth, he blew on it four times and slowly spread it out. He prepared incense. Taking the black cloth by one corner with his left hand while holding the bulk with his right hand, he passed it over the incense smoke four times. He placed the cloth over the wooden bowl, which contained the stuff he had drawn from the patient's body. Then Bull Lodge lit the pipe again and smoke. He blew smoke on the covered bowl four times. Then he stood up with the bowl still covered with black cloth. Holding it up in a gesture of offering he prayed, "Father Above Man, I am grateful for this life you gave me and for these powers to heal and cure. Look down on me. I will raise a body up again." He put the bowl down again and uncovered it. It was empty. The matter in the bowl had mysteriously disappeared. The patient's head was now pointing toward the west. It had first been moved to the east, then to the south, and then towards the final direction. This entire ceremony was one day's doctoring.

Now that Bull Lodge had finished doctoring for the day, he turned his attention to the food which had been prepared for them. He asked for a small piece of meat. When it was given to him, he cut it into four pieces, each the size of a small mouthful. He then called for a small cup of broth. He held these up for the patient to see and asked Yellow Man if it looked inviting. "Yes," said his uncle, "Feed it to me." Then Bull Lodge made incense. Taking the plate which contained the four pieces of meat with his left hand, and the cup with broth in it with his right hand, he held the plate of meat over the incense, then the broth. He raised the plate and cup slightly in a gesture of offering and prayed, "Father Above Man, I am about to feed this food you gave us to a patient who is sick. Look down on us from above as I feed it to my uncle, Yellow Man." After this prayer he sat down and began to feed his uncle.

Bull Lodge took one piece of meat from the plate and held it over the incense, then he held it up for a moment before feeding it to Yellow Man. He took a horn spoon and dipped some of the broth from the cup. He held it up for a moment before putting the spoon to the patient's mouth. Bull Lodge did this until his uncle had eaten all four pieces of meat and drunk all the broth in the cup. Then he turned to to the seven men and six women who sang and said, "All stand up." Bull Lodge stood up as well and told them to raise up their plates of food. While they held their plates of food up, Bull Lodge prayed. "Father Above Man, I am sharing this food you gave me with these people who are in this tipi. Put your kind thoughts into this food from above, that they may enjoy it and have a long life."

Then they all sat down and ate their food together. Now while all these people were eating, the patient was watching them and he thought he would like a little more to eat. So Yellow Man spoke up and said, "My nephew?" "What is it?" Bull Lodge answered. "These people eating makes me want more," said his uncle, "I wish you would give me something more to eat." And hearing this, Yellow Man's father-in-law said, "I am glad that my son-in-law is better already."

Then Bull Lodge took another piece of meat, and breaking a smaller piece off with his fingers, he dipped it in the broth and fed it to his patient. As he passed each piece to his uncle, Bull Lodge would say, "Father Above Man, look down on me as I feed the sick." He did this until Yellow Man had eaten the entire piece of meat he had in his hand. When the meal was over, Bull Lodge distributed the things that were given him for his services as a doctor.

First he gave one horse and one robe to his friend Sits Like A Woman. His niece, Counts Two Coups, received a horse and so did his sister Bird Woman, and his aunt Crane Woman also got a horse. Bull Lodge kept three head of horses and two robes for himself. After distributing the gifts, he said, "Now I am done, so we will all go home. I will go out first, then the men will follow, then the women. All of you will make a complete circle to the left as you go out of the tipi." So he went out first. Then the seven men followed him out, then the six women. When everyone was outside, those who had received horses from Bull Lodge took them away.

The Second Day

It was understood that Bull Lodge was to continue doctoring his sick uncle, and he notified Yellow Man's father-in-law to have the patient ready for him before the sun rose on the second day. So it was done. Before the sun rose, Yellow Man's father-in-law called Bull Lodge and told him the patient was ready. When Bull Lodge went to his uncle's tipi, Yellow Man said to him,"My nephew, I ask you to doctor me just as you were commanded to do. You are to apply the full force of the power given to you as a doctor." "All right, uncle", Bull Lodge answered, "I will do my best." Now the singers remained silent as Bull Lodge began his doctoring. The patient's head was pointed to the west, along with the filled pipe. After the patient was moved, Bull Lodge made incense. Taking his whistle,

Bull Lodge held the mouthpiece of the whistle over the incense, then the opposite end, then the mouthpiece again, then the other end. He incensed both ends of the whistle twice, to make four times. Bull Lodge then circled the patient to his left and stopped at his feet.

Facing away from the patient to the east, Bull Lodge blew long on the whistle. Then he turned to the south without changing his position, and he again blew on the whistle. Turning to the west in the same position, he blew on it again. Then facing the patient, Bull Lodge knelt down, holding the whistle with his left hand as he blew on it once again. This time while blowing the whistle he tapped the sole of the patient's left foot four times. He performed this twice on each foot. After this Bull Lodge stood up and circled the patient, stopping at his head. With the whistle in his left hand he held it to his mouth and blew, meanwhile stroking the patient from his head down to his feet and also shaking his hand gently. He did this four times.

Then Bull Lodge circled the patient, moving to his left and stopped at his feet. He knelt down and took the little fingers of his uncle's hands in both of his own hands and gently shook them. He did this four times, and after each time he would shake the patient's hand and blow breath on him. Then Bull Lodge pulled on all of the patient's fingers, still holding both hands, and popped the joints. Then he pulled on his uncle's fingers once more and raised him to a sitting position, letting go of his hands.

Yellow Man raised his arms high up above his head, as if stretching. He drew his legs up and crossed them. Then the patient placed his hands on his knees as he sat and looked around the tipi. The singers had remained silent during the entire ceremony.

Bull Lodge turned to those present in the tipi. "My relatives," he said, "what you have just witnessed are the results of fasting, hardships, and sacrifices in the past. There are three places in particular where I fasted and was given the power to heal and cure. There was Black Butte, on the south side of the Big River east of Big Spring. There was Grows Tallest Butte in the Many Buttes Mountains and there was the middle butte of the Three Buttes in Canada. Whenever I have pity on someone and doctor him, the performance you witnessed this day is how I bring him back to health.

"It has been revealed to me that you are all to be my children

72

and that your bodies and health are to be under my care. I have hesitated to announce that I would doctor my uncle as many as seven times, and I see now that I shall doctor him only three times, after which he will be able to walk around."

Now that Bull Lodge was through doctoring for the second day, the food was prepared. This time the patient was able to feed himself. The feeding and prayers proceeded just as before. Bull Lodge left the tipi first, then the seven men, then the six women. All made a complete circle to the left as they went out.

The Third Day

The next morning before sunrise, Yellow Man's father-in-law called on Bull Lodge. Bull Lodge told him to prepare the patient by putting his head in the direction of west. The seven men and six women were already at the tipi of the sick man when Bull Lodge entered. He had his drum, wooden bowl, whistle, and black cloth with him. He first made incense and incensed his drum. He held it over the smoke, tipping it down slightly in an easterly direction. Then he tipped it to the south, then to the west, and finally to the north. Next he incensed the bowl, the whistle, and the black cloth. Taking his drum and holding it above his head, he prayed, "My Father, Mountain Man, I am about to use these things that were supernaturally associated with the shield you gave to me. Look down upon me as I perform with them the way you showed me."

After this prayer, Bull Lodge began to sing. After doing the song once for the singers, he asked them to sing it while he doctored. Before they started, Bull Lodge said, "This time, I'll draw with my mouth three times on the patient's chest and three times on his back." As the singers began, Bull Lodge began to draw on the chest of the patient. After he had drawn three times on the chest he ordered the patient turned over, so he could get at the back. But his uncle said, "I don't need any help, I'll turn over on my stomach without help." He did this. Bull Lodge then drew on the back with his mouth. When he finished, the patient turned over again on his back.

Bull Lodge stood up and circled the patient completely, stopping by the patient's side. He took the black cloth and covered the patient with it. He took the wooden bowl and prayed. "My Father, Mountain Man, it was you who appeared to me on the Black Butte. Come to me now and be with me in my first experience as a doctor, I

73

need your help." Then he repeated this short prayer three times with the wooden bowl upraised, and as he did so a slight breath of breeze struck the wooden bowl and his hands. As soon as the breath of breeze came he began to imitate the cry of an eagle. He did this four times. Then he told the patient to uncover his face. After this Bull Lodge placed the bowl on the ground before himself and sat down.

The matter he had drawn out of the patient's chest and back was in the wooden bowl he held as he prayed. But when he put the wooden bowl down, the matter had mysteriously disappeared, and three round objects lay in the bowl instead. Those three objects were only recognizable to Bull Lodge. One was yellow, one dark blue, and the other was red. Each was the size of a large marble, and they lay in a row at the bottom of the bowl. Bull Lodge passed the wooden bowl among the people so that they could inspect the mysterious objects.

Bull Lodge then asked that the patient be helped up, but his uncle said, "I don't need any help, I'll get up by myself." And he did. Then Bull Lodge told the patient to lie down again and he covered him with the black cloth once more. He made incense, and incensed his hands and the wooden bowl while singing his medicine song. After putting down the bowl, Bull Lodge circled the patient, stopping at the left side of the bed nearest the tipi. Then he blew on the whistle four times. Going all the way around the patient's feet he stopped and blew on the whistle four times again, but on the fourth, he blew spasmodically. Bull Lodge circled around the patient's right side and blew his whistle in the same way. Then moving around to the patient's head, he stopped and blew on the whistle again four times. After this he circled around the patient's left side. Grasping the black cloth that was placed over his head, Bull Lodge drew it all the way down the length of his uncle's body, shaking it gently. While he was doing this he said, "Yellow Man arise." He did this four times. After the fourth performance, he said, "All right, Yellow Man, stand up." Slowly, Yellow Man turned onto his right side. Then he got onto his hands and knees, then he stood up in a stooped way, using his hands to brace himself on his knees. The strain of his effort was visible to everyone, but he did not fall. Bull Lodge got down on his knees and told Yellow Man to face in the direction of the rising sun. Then he told his uncle this: "As I move my hands on the ground, you move your feet, first using your right foot while I use my right hand."

Bull Lodge rubbed his hands on the ground gently. Rubbing his palms together he blew his breath on them. Then he said, "All right, Yellow Man, step." With both palms against the ground Bull Lodge moved his right hand forward towards the east, and Yellow Man moved his right foot forward at the same time. Moving his left hand, Bull Lodge said, "Now your left foot." Yellow Man moved his left foot. Then Bull Lodge said to the patient, "Now turn to the south." Yellow Man turned in that direction, and Bull Lodge said, "Now do the same thing again." He moved his right hand on the ground, and Yellow Man moved his right foot. This was done for each of the four directions, so that Yellow Man took two steps in each direction. Then the entire procedure was repeated. Then Bull Lodge told his uncle to sit down on the bed.

Bull Lodge made more incense, and incensed his hands. Kneeling before the patient, he took out one of the three round objects that had appeared in the wooden bowl. He chose the red one. Holding it in his right hand, he motioned away from himself with it and toward the patient. He did this twice with each hand, making it four times. Then he rubbed the object between his hands a few times and stroked the sitting patient from his head to the bed. After dusting his hands, Bull Lodge blew on them then he stroked the patient with his left hand. He repeated this act twice with each hand to make it four times. And Bull Lodge said he was done.

The singers told him the food was ready, and he told them to distribute it, feeding him first. After everyone was served, Bull Lodge told them to stand up and hold their plates high as before while he prayed. Then they all sat down and began to eat. Before taking the first mouthful, each person broke off a small bit of food and placed it on the spot where Bull Lodge made incense.

Then the patient spoke up saying, "I want to eat with you." So Bull Lodge cut four pieces of meat from his share and placed them in his medicine bowl. After holding it up and praying, he gave it to the patient. Bull Lodge told him to pick up a single piece of meat with his right hand and say, "All Powerful, look down on the food your son has shared with me. Make it strengthen me as it comes from his hands." "Now use your left hand," Bull Lodge added, "and so on until you have eaten up all four pieces." The patient ate as Bull Lodge ordered. After everyone had eaten, Bull Lodge said, "We are going now, because I am done for this time."

Bull Lodge got up and started to leave the tipi when his sick uncle, Yellow Man spoke up saying, "I want to go out with you." So he got up and followed Bull Lodge out of the tipi, When they were outside, Bull Lodge said, "Follow me." He led his patient around the tipi, going to his left and circling back to the entrance. Then both of them went back into the tipi. Before Yellow Man sat down he addressed Bull Lodge. "My nephew, you have given life back to me, and I will live it in gratitude to you." Putting his arm around Bull Lodge's neck, he embraced and kissed him. Then Bull Lodge took his leave.

Finishing the Cure

Now the three times Bull Lodge said he would doctor his uncle were completed, and Yellow Man was able to walk again. But not all the work was done. Bull Lodge had to give Yellow Man a drink of medicine four times before he would be completely well. So he went to his uncle's tipi once a day for four days to make the medicine and give it to him. On each of these mid-day visits, Bull Lodge took with him his medicine and the three round colored objects which had appeared mysteriously in the wooden bowl. After making the patient's medicine, Bull Lodge would take one of these objects and stroke him with it. Then he would have his uncle drink the medicine.

On the first of these visits, the medicine was colored yellow, on the second it was colored dark blue, and on the third it was made from hailstone water, which was green. The color appeared as soon as the medicine touched the water. On the fourth visit Bull Lodge made a colorless water, using the supernatural powers that were given to him. Each visit, he covered his wooden bowl with the black cloth and sang his medicine song four times. Then he lit his pipe and blew the smoke on the covered bowl four times. He raised the cloth from the wooden bowl and saw that there was now water in it. Taking a pinch of medicine between his thumb and forefinger, he sprinkled a little bit in four different places in the container of water. He said a silent prayer as he held up the medicine, then he dropped the rest of it into the water. It was now ready for the patient to drink. By this time, Yellow Man was far advanced in recovering from his sickness. After he had drunk the medicine on the fourth day, Bull Lodge pronounced him cured.

The work of Bull Lodge occurred when he had reached the age

of forty, and it was the first of his doctoring experiences. He then doctored six other persons in the same way as for his uncle, until he reached the number seven. After the first seven cases, he doctored twelve persons a different way. This is how Bull Lodge explained the significance of this.

"The first seven I doctored signified the seven buttes I fasted on during my experiences seeking the manhood I desired. The next twelve I doctored signified my age when I was first contacted by the supernatural. The seven men and six women who sang also means something. Their number signifies the days in the duration of my fasting experience. I stayed on the first butte for seven days and nights, on the second butte six days and nights, on the third butte five days and nights, and so on until the seventh and last butte, where I only stayed one day and one night. So the first seven times that I doctored, fewer and fewer singers were used, representing the decreasing number of days and nights on each butte that I fasted. I continued this until I had decreased the number to four men and three women. I kept that number for my permanent use, to sing for me whenever I doctored my best and hardest.

"After I had doctored the first seven in the manner I told to you, I doctored the next twelve a different way, without using the singers. In all of those first nineteen patients, I did not lose one. They were all successfully performed."

A short time after Bull Lodge's first nineteen cases of doctoring, he was given the Chief Medicine Pipe called The Feathered Pipe, which he had worshipped since his childhood. Giving Bull Lodge the Chief Medicine Pipe also conferred upon him the sacred office of medicine man, and with a special ceremony he was given the title of Chief Medicine Man. Bull Lodge was now a medicine man, a noted doctor, and a brave warrior. He was greatly respected among the people. He was held as one of the greatest men of the tribe, and he made good use of his powers.

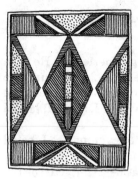

3. MEDICINE MAN, PIPE KEEPER, FATHER

Four days after I was born, Bull Lodge was given the Chief Medicine Pipe which is called the Feathered Pipe. It greatly increased his prestige among the Gros Ventre people. I was alive during the following healing performances of my father, and I witnessed some of them.

The Healing of Little Swallow

There was a battle between the Sioux and the Crows in the neighborhood of Big Mountain Sheep River, which is still Crow country, and a Crow warrior named Little Swallow was wounded. He was charging along the enemy line when a Sioux bullet caught him, entering just above his right hip bone and passing out of his left side below the navel. He was on horseback and managed to make it back to the Crow line. After the battle he was carried back to camp. At that time Bull Lodge was camping with the Crows, for peace had just been made between our people and the Crow tribe.[1]

Bull Lodge was formally called to doctor the wounded man. When he entered the lodge, he saw at a glance that Little Swallow was in bad shape. It was clear that he couldn't be expected to live much longer. Immediately Bull Lodge ordered that water be heated. While he waited, he took out his black cloth, holding one corner with his right hand and the balance in his left hand. He stood before Little Swallow and made a rising motion with the black cloth. He did this three more times. He had sipped some water before performing this, and each time he motioned, he sent a fine spray of water from his mouth onto the patient. Seeing that Little Swallow was getting weaker fast and that his eyes were turning up, Bull Lodge drew the black cloth down along the patient's face, from forehead to chin. He performed this four times. He did it to keep his patient's eyes properly focused. After this, Little Swallow looked around the lodge.

By this time the water had been heated. Bull Lodge took a pinch of medicine from a small log. He sprinkled some in at four different places in his bowl of water. Holding the rest of the medicine between finger and thumb, he made a silent prayer. Then he put all the medicine in the water and it turned blue instantly.

Bull Lodge made incense. Afterwards, he held his drum in his left hand while he gently rubbed the palm of his right hand on the ground. He guided his right hand around the entire rim of the drum. Then he held the drum over the burning incense, exposing four different places to it by turns at the rim. Then he held the drum above him for a moment.

He untied the piece of cloth which connected the drum stick to the drum and held the tied end over incense with his right hand. Then he held it above his head. He made a gesture with the stick as though he were going to strike the drum, but he did not complete it. He repeated this motion three times. The fourth time, he completed the strike. Then he held the drum stick up and prayed, "My Father, Above Man, look down upon me. A human body is in pain. Take care of it. I am about to strike our drum. May I drive the pain away with the sound of the drum."

1. After this peace was made, a friendship sprung up between the two peoples. There were intermittent periods of strife and friendship throughout this period. During times of peace, the tribes intermingled both ways, even to the extent of frequent intermarriage.

Then he began to drum and sing his healing song. He sang it four times, then he turned the drumming and singing over to his four assistants. He turned to his patient, and ordered his wife to wash his wounds with the medicine he had made, using buffalo hair as cotton. When this had been done, Little Swallow was turned on his left side to expose the wound. Dipping the buffalo hair in his medicine, Bull Lodge held it to the wound and squeezed it so that medicine would run into the wound. Little Swallow was positioned so that the medicine would run through his body along the course the bullet made. Bull Lodge performed this four times.

Then he cut two small pieces from a section of tanned buffalo bladder that he always kept on hand. They were big enough to cover the entrance and exit wounds of the bullet. He told his wife to incense her hands and place the pieces of buffalo bladder over Little Swallow's wounds. But his wife said, "This is not my work. You do it yourself."

Bull Lodge spat on his index finger four times and dipped it into the medicine. Then he applied the strip of bladder to one of Little Swallow's wounds. He took the other piece of bladder and did the same, to cover both wounds. He told the patient to drink all the dark blue medicine from the cup.

This was all Bull Lodge did the first time. He told Little Swallow's relative he would be all right. He said he would doctor Little Swallow once more, and he would be well then.

The next day Bull Lodge doctored Little Swallow in the same manner, except that he grafted new skin over the two wounds where the bullet had passed. He pulled off the bladder skins he had applied the previous day. Then he dipped the buffalo hair into the medicine and dripped it into the wound so that it ran through the wound into the patient's belly. He did this four times. He gave Little Swallow the medicine to drink. Then he cut two small pieces of the bladder skin and placed the pieces over the wounds in the same manner as the day before. But this time he used the black cloth to cover the wounds.

Bull Lodge then lit a pipe filled with kinnickinnic. He blew the smoke on the wounds while they were covered with the black cloth. He did this twice for each wound, making four times in all. Then he removed the cloth from Little Swallow's belly, to show the people present. Not a trace of a scar remained on Little Swallow's body. Bull Lodge's doctoring was finished.

Little Swallow lived to a ripe old age. If the reputation of Bull Lodge as a medicine man had not been known, Little Swallow would not have seen the sun go down the day the Sioux shot him.

The Healing of the Crow Child

I saw my father use his power to cure another time while he was still among the Crows. There was a ten year-old girl who was hemorrhaging through her mouth. Her parents called my father to stop the blood, and my mother and I went along. When we arrived, the child was already weak from loss of blood. The girl's name was Braided Hair and her father's name was White Neck.

When we entered White Neck's lodge, the girl was being held by her father and mother. She was vomiting blood and her parents were under a terrible strain. They saw their daughter suffering and they were helpless to console her. Immediately they implored my father to do something for their daughter. Their pleas and the sight of Braided Hair's condition touched my father to the quick.

Immediately he ordered fresh water to be brought from the running stream. He commanded that the bucket be dipped into the water against the natural flow of the stream. But while this was being done, Bull Lodge saw that something had to be done for the child immediately. He took his cup and dipped water from a bucket that was handy. He took a sip of the water and stood before the child just to her right. He blew a fine spray of water onto the right side of the child's neck. He circled around the back of the child to her left, where he stopped and blew water onto that side of her neck. Then Bull Lodge took out his black cloth and wrapped it around Braided Hair's neck. He left it there while waiting for the fresh water. The child had now stopped vomiting, and blood had ceased to come out of her mouth.

When the fresh water came, Bull Lodge dipped some out with a horn spoon. My mother held the horn spoon for him while he took some medicine out of his small bag. He took a pinch of the medicine between his thumb and index finger and put it in the water in the horn spoon. The water instantly turned red.

Bull Lodge took a sip of the red medicine and removed the black cloth from the child. He stood before her to her right and blew a fine spray onto the right side of her neck. He moved around behind her, stopping at her left side and blew a fine spray onto the right side of her neck. Then Bull Lodge held the black cloth bunched on top of her head. He drew it down her back until the cloth touched the place where she was sitting. Shaking it gently in a dusting gesture, he moved to the other side and drew the black cloth down her front. Then he shook it gently again.

By now the child was resting comfortably.

Bull Lodge touched his right arm, at a point just above the elbow, to the same point on the girl's right arm. It was as though he were making some mark, but it was only a formal gesture. He did the same thing with his left arm upon her left arm. Then he quickly drew his black cloth completely around her neck.

Bull Lodge pronounced Braided Hair cured then. She was never troubled with hemorrhages again. She lived for many years, although she would have died that very day had not Bull Lodge helped her.

Bull Lodge was given two horses, two blankets, one gun scabbard and two parfleches for his services. The total number of these things represented the seven buttes where he had fasted while seeking his manhood.

The Crows Slight Garter Snake and Regret It

Another time I remember seeing my father perform by using his power to control the rain. I was only three years old then, but I remember it because I was the cause of it all. We were camping with the Crows, and my father became angry because I was not given any of the buffalo tongue served at a great feast before the sun dance began.

I remember that I cried and fussed so much at being passed over, my mother decided to take me back to the lodge. Bull Lodge had some Crow visitors. They were all sitting in a half circle just outside the tipi, and a pipe filled with kinnickinnic was being passed back and forth. When my mother came up with me so upset, my father was alarmed. I was his favorite child, and he was always concerned about even my smallest hurts.

My mother said I was pouting because the Crows did not feed my any buffalo tongue at the feast. Then my father sat in silence for a bit with his head bowed. When he raised his head he told my mother to enter the tipi, then he stood up and motioned his Crow visitors inside as well. The names of the Crows who followed him in were Large Bear, Crazy Head, Crooked Arm, and Raven Woman (also known as Sits In The Middle).

Bull Lodge immediately made incense. Then he held the top covering of the Chief Medicine Pipe called the Feathered Pipe over the incense. (The top covering of the bundle is made from a thick, heavy cloth called list cloth.) He called for water and my mother brought him some in a cup. He sipped it a little, then he raised the list cloth by two corners and held it up to the west, although he was within the tipi. He motioned with the cloth as though he were beckoning to the west. Then he turned to the east and shook the cloth gently, as though he were shaking something off. He performed this four times.

Bull Lodge then sat down and talked to the Crows by signs. Because the Crow people had not fed his daughter, Garter Snake Woman, he said, it would rain for four days and nights. It would hinder the progress of their sun dance and perhaps ruin the entire ceremony. Then he asked one of the Crows to step out and look to the west, to see if any clouds had appeared. The Crow man did this and returned saying that clouds were already coming close, and that he could see the lightning play across the sky.

In no time a terrific electric storm struck the camp. Water was running everywhere. The clouds had burst!

Crooked Arm and Raven Woman went out to find Sore Lips, the Crow who was organizing the sun dance. They told him what Bull Lodge had said, and why he had interfered with the sun dance by calling the rain. Sore Lips called his closest relatives together, and they all went back to Bull Lodge's tipi. They carried a pipe filled with kinnickinnic, a blanket, two robes, and a number of cooked buffalo tongues to give to the pouting child. Entering the tipi, Sore Lips approached Bull Lodge with the filled pipe extended before him. He implored him to stop the rain. He said that they had been wrong not to feed his favorite child, but that it was not done intentionally. It was a careless oversight by the men who were passing the food around. He begged Bull Lodge's forgiveness.

Then Bull Lodge took the filled pipe and lit it and began to smoke, which was a sign of acceptance. Looking at Sore Lips while pointing to me, he said, "This is my favorite child. I am very attached to her because she has been a sickly one and I have had a hard time with her health. So when she came home crying because my friends had not fed her, my heart was wounded. I proceeded to punish your people by making bad weather during the sun dance ceremony."

Then Bull Lodge made incense. He took his drum down and held it over the incense, then he sang his medicine song, keeping time with the drum. When he had sung it three times, everyone noticed that the sound of rainfall on the tipi was lessening. When he had sung it a fourth time, he called for his eagle wing fan.

My mother took the eagle wing down from where it was hanging in the tipi. Bull Lodge held it over the incense for a moment, then drew it away. He did this four times. Then he stood up and faced towards the west, holding the eagle wing outstretched before him in his right hand, slightly higher than head level. He held the wing from the end, where it joins the eagle's body, and he kept its tips pointing up, perpendicular to the ground. He motioned to his right with the wing, then he returned it to the point before him, then he passed the wing to the left. He repeated this three more times, gesturing first to the right with the wing, then to the left. Thus he motioned four times in all with the eagle wing, and when he had finished he sat down.

He asked one of the Crows to go out and look at the sky. The man reported that the clouds in the west were parting, half drifting north and half drifting south. A short time later the rain stopped completely and the sun came out. So the sun dance was allowed to continue to its completion.

The Gift of the Painted Tipi

Within a two year period, my father had the same dream four times. A small boy approached him and told him that he would be given a painted tipi. And Bull Lodge would answer "Yes" in the dream. In the fourth dream the little boy described the tipi that would be given to him, and Bull Lodge said, "All right, give the tipi to me. I am ready for it."

The following spring the tribe moved its camp to Beaver Creek, which is just east of the Fur Cap Mountains, or Little Rockies. They were hunting for buffalo for meat and hides, which was the custom at that season. Hides were especially needed for tipis. From Beaver Creek the tribe moved northward around the edge of the mountains to Little Warm Creek, where they made some tipis. Then they moved west along the foothills of the Fur Cap Mountains to Red Mountain Creek, which is now known as Lodge

Pole Creek. The tribe camped there only long enough to tan hides and make a few more tipis. Then they followed the course of Red Mountain Creek to where it joins Little People's Creek. They camped just above the fork of the creek, straight east of Little Moccasin Buttes (now known as Three Buttes, Montana), where more buffalo were killed for their hides and meat.

The tribe moved with the course of Little People's Creek and camped directly south of Little Moccasin Butte. It was at this place that Bull Lodge made a new tipi. It was very large, requiring eighteen hides. From there the tribe moved straight west and camped near the place called the Circle of Cliffs, now known as Sand Cliffs. During the night an electrical storm came and passed off after midnight.

Bull Lodge awoke before sunrise. He told his family to go outside and look at the tipi. He had a vision that night during the storm. When his wife returned she said the the tipi was now painted. Bull Lodge called an old man named Butte, and told him to cry out about this mysterious event. So the old man went through the entire camp, crying the news to the people and telling them to get up and see the tipi.

There were four designs on the tipi. About three feet from the bottom and extending around the tipi was an imitation of a rainbow, painted black, red, yellow and white. A black disc had been painted on each side of the tent flaps, just even with the lower end of the flap. Each disc had a small light blue circle in its center, about two inches across. And like a cross behind each disc, four colored lines were painted, colored black, red, yellow and white. High up on the back side of the tipi, about three feet from the top of the cover was a black bird about the size of a magpie, with outstretched wings. The edge of the entrance was painted red, about a foot wide all around, and the hide that served as a door was also red, as well as the stick tied across the center of the hide to keep it outspread.

Later Bull Lodge was told in a vision that he should make a new tipi like this every year until he had made four of them. He was instructed to paint them exactly like this one. The following year Bull Lodge made the first one early in the summer, when the tribe was camped on the Little River, just below the place where Snake Creek empties into it. Sitting High, Black Bird, Crooked Arm and Otter Robe were appointed by Bull Lodge to paint the tipi.

They spread out the new tipi in order to work on it, using a stick to measure the distances where the paint was to go.

But Bull Lodge was unable to fulfill the command given him in his vision, because the buffalo disappeared after he finished his second tipi. He was forced to abandon his obligation to make the other two tipis, which would have completed the series of four.

Bull Lodge Heals With the Woodpecker Feather

About once a year my father would have a vision reminding him of the woodpecker he was given for operations on patients who had tumors. The fourth time he had this vision, he was told that whenever he put his hand into the patient's body through the cut place, his hand would turn into a woodpecker.

One day, when the tribe was camped on the Little River near the present site of Chinook, Montana, a man named White Bird came to Bull Lodge and formally called upon him to doctor his wife Windy Woman, who had a tumor. Bull Lodge asked White Bird what he intended to give him for his services. "There is my herd of horses," said White Bird. "You can take as many as you want."

"I'll take seven head," Bull Lodge replied.

Then he told White Bird to position the patient's head so that it pointed east. He instructed him to fill a pipe with kinnickinnic and lay it so that the stem pointed in the same direction as the patient's head. He told him he must provide seven men and five women to do the singing. "My wife will be the sixth woman singing," he added.

White Bird went home and did as Bull Lodge ordered. He called the following men to be singers: Breath, Comes Flying, Many Fold, Crooked Arm, Crazy Bull, Red Whip and Otter Robe. The women he called were Hiding Woman, Homely, Black Eyes, Digger, Good Kill, and One Woman, who was the wife of Bull Lodge.

Bull Lodge went to White Bird's tipi with his medicine kit made of wolverine tanned skin and his drum. He took his place beside the patient, Windy Woman, and made incense. Then he made medicine in his wooden bowl. He ripped the patient's dress down the back and had it lowered to expose her abdomen. He covered her face and abdomen with his black cloth. He called her husband over and asked him to show him where the tumor was. Bull Lodge then lifted the cloth, took a piece of charcoal and made a vertical mark about six inches long over the place. Then he held his drum over the incense, after which he sang his medicine song. He sang it three times, then he turned the drumming and singing over to the singers.

Bull Lodge took the woodpecker feathers out and blew his breath on them four times. Then he incensed a single wing feather. He raised the black cloth again, just far enough to expose the marked place on the patient's abdomen, then he slid a woodpecker wing feather over it in a brushing gesture. He did this four times. All this time the people were singing Bull Lodge's medicine songs.

After blowing on the feather four times, he stuck the tip in the medicine he had made in the wooden bowl, and he applied it to the upper end of the charcoal mark on the abdomen. Then he imitated the call of the woodpecker. Instantly the woodpecker feather entered the abdomen. It was like a knife being driven in. The feather entered to about half its length, and Bull Lodge began to draw it down along the course of the black mark. The sound of the progress of the feather through flesh was like the sound of a knife. The feather entered the mark at the top, close to the chest, and it was drawn down to the end of the mark.

Then Bull Lodge took the feather out and incensed each hand twice. Holding the cut open with his left hand, he put his right hand into it. He took out a round object which just fitted the palm of his hand with his fingers cupped. He laid it in the wooden bowl, then took up one of the feathers. After holding it over the incense and incensing his hand as well, he scraped the blood back into the cut. Then he covered the abdomen with the black cloth.

Bull Lodge took up the pipe that was lying there for his use, filled with kinnickinnic. Holding it with his left hand, the pipe stem pointing toward himself, he rubbed his right palm on the ground gently and stroked the pipe. He started each stroke from the pipe end, coming towards the stem and himself. Then he changed the pipe to his right hand and performed the same actions with his left hand. He repeated this with each hand, to make it four times in all that he stroked the pipe. With the filled pipe in both hands, he then held it to his mouth and sucked on the stem. He blew his breath over and directly above the pipe. Sucking once more he blew his breath below and directly under the filled pipe. Then he performed the same act again, blowing first above then below. Finally he lit the pipe and began to smoke. He blew smoke upon the black cloth directly over the cut on the patient's abdomen. When he had blown smoke on the cloth four times, he raised it. All that could be seen on the body was a small streak, like a little scratch, where the cut had been.

Bull Lodge took a pinch of ashes from the incense. Putting them in the palm of his left hand, he ground them fine with his right index finger. Then he blew his breath on the ashes four times and sprinkled them upon the scar on the patient's abdomen. He took the woodpecker tail feather and blew his breath on it four times, then he held it over the incense. With his right hand he slid the feather down over the scar, toward the feet. He did this four times. Then he took the black cloth and incensed it four times, at the same time blowing on his whistle. He stroked the patient once from the chest down past the abdomen. Then he shook the cloth in a dusting gesture and stopped the singers. This meant he had finished doctoring.

Windy Woman said she felt tired but wanted to sit up. "You can sit up," said Bull Lodge. And she sat up for a while.

Now the seven horses Bull Lodge took from White Bird's herd represent the seven buttes where he had fasted. At the time of the healing of Windy Woman, Bull Lodge still owned the Chief Medicine Pipe called the Feathered Pipe. A few years after this, he gave the Feathered Pipe to a man named Sitting High.

In the next story, which is the fourth part of Bull Lodge's life history and its closing chapter, he is without the title connected with the Chief Medicine Pipe. Nevertheless, Bull Lodge was a medicine man for the rest of his life. As I will show, he was directly connected with the supernatural right up to the night he died.

4. THE LAST EXPERIENCE

This is the fourth and last part of Bull Lodge's life history. In this final narrative, Garter Snake Woman tells us how her father was granted the power of resurrection if the ceremony of Four Sweat Tents were properly performed, but that it could not be done because the buffalo were gone. She tells how the seven great men of the other world sat in judgment upon his case, and how these judges were divided, with a majority in favor of taking him away, and how their messenger revealed this verdict to Bull Lodge. Thus he learned the exact number of days remaining to him. Finally she recalls the courageous way her father endured his final ordeal, displaying a perfect resignation to his fate.

While telling these things, Garter Snake Woman was reliving the saddest experiences of her life. It took longer for her to get through than any of the other parts. Especially at the close, she was slowed by overpowering emotions as she relived her own and her father's experience. Garter Snake Woman was the most beloved person in the family and her father's favorite.

As she spoke the words I have recorded here, they were mingled with tears. At times she stopped talking altogether, and I looked up from the paper to see her lips moving in silent prayer. She was asking for strength and courage to go on with her telling. When the pressure was too great, she knelt and blessed herself with the sign of the cross and prayed aloud for divine help, that she might not fail in performing her task, despite her old age. But Garter Snake Woman stood the test. When she had finished, she breathed a sigh of relief. She sat with her eyes closed for a long time. Then she raised her head and told me, "You have put me to a severe test. The end of the story I have told you was the most painful time I ever experienced."

The Gift of the Four Sweat Tents

One spring night Bull Lodge had a vision in his sleep. An old man stood at a distance on the horizon of a low hill to the east. It was just before sunrise, because the old man stood in plain view with the sun's glow behind him. And as Bull Lodge watched, the person came towards him and stopped beside him. The old man wore everyday Indian clothes, but what particularly drew Bull Lodge's attention was his hair and cane. The old man had long snow-white hair and the upper part of his head was covered with the dark red paint traditionally used by the Gros Ventres. His cane was also painted with this sacred paint.

Then the old man spoke to Bull Lodge, "I came to tell you of my life. I give it to you. You will live until you die of old age, but before that time you will pass away so that you may demonstrate the power I am giving you, the power to rise after you have passed away. I give you four sweat tents which are to be made after you pass away. These sweat tents are to be built one behind the other facing east. They will stand in a line running east and west. The first sweat tent must have twenty willows for its frame, the next one eighteen, the next sixteen, and the fourth and last tent must have fourteen willows. The first tent will stand at the east end, the fourth at the west end.

"These tents are to be spaced just far enough apart so that there is room between them to pass from one to the other. Your body is to be carried to the first sweat tent by four men. They will lay your body down in the tent. Then one of them is to make incense for you with sweet pine needles. The four men will then go out, two through the entrance and the other two through the back. When they are outside they will lower the covering of the sweat tent and sing this song." (The old man sang it to Bull Lodge.) "They must sing this four times, then return to the places where they came out of the sweat tent, at the front and back. The two at the back will then raise the tent cover and enter. They will carry your body to the second sweat tent and the ceremony will be repeated there. After the second performance your body will be carried into the third sweat tent and laid there, and the same performance will take place as in the two before it. In the third sweat tent you will move a little. Then you will be carried into the fourth and last sweat tent. I will be present there, and after the singing is done I will speak to you, saying, 'Sits Fast, arise and come out.' Then you will come out of the fourth and last sweat tent, alive again."

When the old man had finished telling all this to Bull Lodge, he handed his cane to him. He said nothing more, but began to rise from the ground. As Bull Lodge stood watching, the old man rose a short distance into the air and changed into a bird, although Bull Lodge could not tell what kind. He watched it until it disappeared from sight. After this Bull Lodge called together those who were closest to him and told them what had been revealed in the vision. Those who were present then were Star Robe, Sits Like A Woman, Sitting High, Black Bird, Bear Travel On Side Hill, Black Sun, White Cow Stripped, and Bull Lodge's family, so that I too was present.

The Judgment of the Council of Seven

A year later, the following spring, Bull Lodge had another vision in his sleep. A messenger came to tell him he was wanted up above, and that seven great men were sitting in council on his case. He said that a dispute arose as to whether Bull Lodge was to be taken away from the earth or not. Four of the council members wanted to take him away and three were in favor of leaving him here on earth. The three great men who wanted to leave Bull Lodge on earth said he was needed by his people here, but the four who wanted to take him away said his work on earth was finished, and that he was needed where he was to go. These councils took place from time to time throughout that spring and summer. After each council, the same messenger came to Bull Lodge with news about it, telling how those who wanted to take him away would not give in to the three who wanted to keep him on earth.

The seventh council was held late that fall. The messenger told Bull Lodge that those who wanted to take him away had won over those who wanted him to remain there. Bull Lodge was calm about this. He was perfectly resigned to their will. One night after winter set in, he was told in a vision that his time on earth was done, that he was allowed exactly eight more days to live. When he awoke in the morning, he took a piece of charcoal from the fireplace and made a mark on a white cloth fastened to the tipi pole behind his bed. The black mark was about six inches long, like the figure one. Each morning after he awoke he would make another mark. On the sixth day a man named Wolf was contacted, at Bull Hook on the Little River. Bull Lodge asked him to tell his son Curly Head to return home to be with his father when he passed away. The tribe was then camped on the Little River where Lohman, Montana now stands. Curly Head arrived the next day, the seventh day according to the marks on the white cloth. That evening Bull Lodge called in all his sons and daughters and an old man named White Porcupine, and he talked to them. He spoke first to Otter Robe, cautioning him about us, his sisters, saying, "Don't you take their horses away from them, they are married and raising children."

Then to Curly Head he said, "Be kind to your sisters and their mother. Remember, she raised you from the time your own mother died. Always stand by her for the rest of her life." After Bull Lodge had finished talking to us and telling us to love one another, he began to tell us about all that had taken place in his visions and what had been revealed to him. He also explained the marks he put on the white cloth, that they told when he was going to leave us.

"I am calling you together here to tell you what is to take place soon. I can't help it. My father wants me, but I don't know what for. I am told that my time of this earth is done and that I can't help myself, for I must obey the commands of Those Who Watch Over Me. The three who wanted me to be left here on this earth tried their best to hold me, but the four who wanted to take me away were more numerous and overruled them." Then he told us to go home and go to bed, and everyone who was present left for their tipis, except for myself and the old man, White Porcupine. But my father said, "Daughter, you had better go to your tipi and your man and go to bed."

I went home, but I could not sleep, my heart was so heavy with grief at what my father had told us. Every concern was driven from me but my father. I got up early the next morning and went to my father's tipi, where I stayed all day. I lost my appetite, and the tears kept gushing out during the day as I sat there. Whenever I returned to our tipi my husband tried to soothe me, but nothing would help. When I entered my father's tipi early that morning I looked at the white cloth behind his bed and I saw the eighth and last mark which he put there himself. It meant that this was his last day with us here on earth.

Telling War Stories

That evening all of his sons and daughters were there early, and the old man White Porcupine was also called to be present. When he arrived, everyone ate but me. I could not eat anything. After the meal, my father told a war story to White Porcupine, in which he and his friend Sits Like A Woman took part. In fact, Sits Like A Woman was leading that particular war party.

I had just stepped out, and when I reentered the tipi, my father was telling about how an owl had helped that war party escape after a surprise raid.

"We had already settled for the night. We had made a temporary shelter out of dead falls of small poles, brush and rye grass and had a fire going, when out of the near brush we heard an owl hoot. This owl would say my name, then he would hoot. After the owl had repeated this two or three times, I told my friend, 'That owl is saying my name.' So Sits Like A Woman called a retreat. 'Get your things together,' he said, 'and we'll get out of here. That owl isn't doing that for nothing.' So we all left as carefully as we could without making noise. The night was cloudy and exceptionally dark. So that no one would stray off, Sits Like A Woman ordered us to hold onto one another's hands. We had camped on a small stream some distance away from the mountains and Sits Like A Woman led us to them. We came to a rock cliff, looked around, found a nice secluded spot and sat down to wait for the early dawn.

"After a while, we noticed dirt and small rocks rolling toward us. One of the men said, 'I'll look around,' and went up along the cliff a ways. Pretty soon he shot his gun. Then we heard something rolling near where we sat and it rolled on past us. No one moved or seemed to pay any attention. The man returned and sat down. When daylight came so that we could see pretty well, one of the men went to the place where we heard the rolling stop. We called. 'It's a mountain goat,' he said. By then the light enabled us to see quite a ways. Suddenly we heard a commotion at the spot where we had stopped earlier that night. Shots could be heard, and war cries and yells. Then the noise stopped. They must have discovered there was no one there. We watched them ride away and recognized them as Crows. When they had gone, we butchered the mountain goat and had a big feast. Sits Like A Woman ordered the blood saved, so one of the men scooped the blood into a paunch which served as a bucket.

"This is how we used the goat skin to make our blood soup. We tied four sticks into a square shape and put the goat skin over them, pushing the hide down inside the square of sticks to form a hollow. The blood was poured into the hollow and some rocks were heated. When they were red hot, two of them were put into the hollow along with some peeled green willow sticks. The hot rocks were pushed around in the blood. When they cooled they were replaced by two more heated rocks. This continued until the blood was cooked. The heated rocks were continually stirred so that the blood soup would cook evenly. Those rocks won't burn hide."

After my father finished telling this, he ordered lunch. We ate, then we daughters took lunches to our husbands, as is the Gros Ventre custom. My mother never spoke a word all this time. She was bearing her grief silently. Bull Lodge told my mother to fix their grandchild. He meant for her to rebundle my baby. My mother handed it to him and he kissed it and said her name, Mountain Sleep. "This poor child will not know me," he said. "She will only hear of my name." Then he laid her on the pillow on his bed, and called for my sister's baby also. He spoke her name, Short Face, and kissed her, then he laid her on his pillow beside Mountain Sleep.

This was the night my father was to die. He told many stories of his past escapades and of the thrilling adventures he had experienced, as though he were reviewing his life.

I still remember one story he told that night. It was of the famous Gros Ventre warrior, Bob Tail Horse. He had acquired that name because he always rode a black bob-tailed horse for his exploits against enemy tribes. But his true name was Scaley, meaning rough skin. It seems that once he was set afoot up in Piegan country, and had to walk home through the heat of the summer.

"We had raided the Piegan camp," said my father, "and it was a success, but Bob Tail Horse was not satisfied. He entered the camp again and was caught, so we had to leave him. He had brought it on himself. The Piegans surrounded him in the brush, but he managed to slip through them by leaving his horse and going on foot. In his getaway he came to a lake full of tall water weeds near the shore. He waded out into the lake, walking backwards and straightening the water weeds he parted as he walked through them, to hide his track. He waded all the way across and went into the brush on the other side. The Piegans surrounded the lake and built fires all around it, but he had already slipped through. Bob Tail Horse then started for home afoot. He wanted to get as far away as he could before daylight.

"He traveled mostly at night until he was far from the enemy's territory. But being unable to choose his path at night, his moccasins didn't last long. His feet became full of raw sores. He tore his clothes in strips to wrap around his feet, but soon he ran out of material and had to crawl. When his hands and knees wore down to sores he tried to think of other ways to move. He even wore his seat out, and his elbows, but he managed to keep on. At night the mosquitoes gave him no rest and he had nothing to eat except what he could pick up around him.

"Bob Tail Horse was gone most of the early summer, and his father and mother were upset about his absence. They asked for details from those who had gone with him. They were ready to leave, they said, but Bob Tail Horse returned to the Piegan camp. They had waited and heard a commotion in the camp with some shots fired. They said they knew he was caught, so they left him.

"Bob Tail Horse was the son of Deer and Hiding Woman. These people appealed to the medicine men to exercise their powers and find out whether their son was dead or alive. The medicine men directed them to White Clothes, an old woman who was noted among the Gros Ventre people for her power to communicate with the spirit world. She consented and performed the ceremony of communication with the Spirit. In it the Spirit said, 'He is not at the spirit world, so he must be still here. I'll look around for him. Give me a little time before you sing again.' When the old woman sang her medicine song again, the Spirit came and said Bob Tail Horse was about a day's travel away, in bad physical condition. The Spirit said, 'In the morning go up onto the first ridge to the west and wait there. Just a little after the sun rises you will see Bob Tail Horse come up on the next ridge west.'

"The parents did as they were told. Sure enough, after the sun was up they saw him coming over the next ridge. Some of the young men rode on horseback to him, observed his condition and told him to wait there. They hurried back and told his parents to go after him with a travois, which was done. The tribe was camped just south of where Chinook now stands. Bob Tail Horse was confined for a long time healing from the sores he developed on his trip home on foot. When he was well again, he set out to take revenge upon the Piegans for setting him afoot.

"On his first warpath trip back to the Piegan country, he hid his horse near their camp. It was broad daylight. Soon he saw a Piegan leaving the camps and he waylaid him when the Piegan got close enough. Seeing him the Piegan spoke, but Bob Tail Horse immediately shot him in the head, killing him. After scalping him and leaving him there, he got away without the tribe knowing. Only later did someone find the victim, after the dogs had begun eating the body.

"On his second trip back to Piegan country, Bob Horse Tail shot and killed a Piegan right on the outskirts of the camp. After shooting the warrior off his horse, Bob Tail Horse took the horse and made a safe getaway. This time he was recognized by the Piegans.

"Bob Tail Horse made a third trip back, and had penetrated into the camp when he found a horse picketed near a tipi. He started to cut it loose when he was seen. The Piegan said, 'What are you doing?' Instead of answering, Bob Tail Horse shot the Piegan, mounted the horse and made a break for safety. But the Piegans were out and aroused, and someone took a shot at him as he raced away. The bullet struck Bob Tail Horse just above his right hip bone and went clear through him, but he did not fall off his horse. He made good his escape and made it to where the war party was waiting for him.

"When they discovered he had been shot, they put him on a horse and started home with him. It was winter, and when Bob Tail Horse asked for water, the party had to stop and melt snow for him to drink. When he drank the water, they could see it running out through the wound where the bullet had left his body. Before they got him home, Bob Tail Horse died. They buried him right where he died, on Little River above Bull Hook."

Farewells

When my father finished telling this story, he began talking about the Feathered Pipe. "I am the last man of those four," he said, "whom the first owner of the Feathered Pipe had foretold would be blessed with its supernatural powers. There is no longer any rule connected with the Chief Medicine Pipe called the Feathered Pipe to guide its existence in the tribe. At one time it was decided that every sixteenth man would receive the great powers supernaturally, until four had received them. This has come to pass. Since I was the last of those four men, the Feathered Pipe and its purpose for the tribe has run its course. There can be no more supernatural powers attached to it. I pity my son the Feathered Pipe, for its days are ended. It shall change hands no more than two or three times after me."

After he finished telling this to us, Bull Lodge asked Long Hair to go outside and look at the stars called the Bulls, which are spaced evenly in a horizontal line. He also asked to know the position of the seven stars called The Dipper. Long Hair came back into the tipi and said that both the three stars and the Dipper were high. Then my father said to Long Hair, "You may not be believed, so I'll go outside and see for myself." He got up and went out. He was gone only a short while, then returned and came to me saying, "My poor daughter." Then he kissed me and went to his wife and kissed her. Then he went to my younger sister and after kissing her he went across to the other side of the tipi where the men sat. He shook Otter Robe's hand and kissed him, then he went to his other son, Curly Head, and shook his hand and kissed him.

Then Bull Lodge shook hands with all the others who were present. He told his wife to rebundle their grandchildren, and when she had done this she brought them in turn and he kissed them both and placed them on the pillow on his bed. Then he took down his medicine bag made of wolverine skin and took some small bags out of it. He turned to his wife and said, "Look carefully at these bags of medicine." He told her what each was for, one by one, until he had laid them all out in a row before him. There were seven small bags of medicine lying there. Much of the medicine in them was finely ground up. But there also were four medicines in whole root form in each of the seven bags, making twenty-eight pieces of medicine still in their natural form. Bull Lodge told his wife, "Keep these for our daughter, Garter Snake Woman. When she has reached her fiftieth year of age, you are to give these medicines to her. She can use them from that time on."

Then he called me and I got up and went to him. He told me to kneel before him. He made incense, then he took his black doctoring cloth, holding it by one corner with his left hand. He stroked its full length with his right hand, then he moved the cloth to the other hand and stroked it once more. He repeated this twice with each hand. Then, after holding the black cloth over the incense for a short time, he covered my head with it and left it there for a little while. Then he took the black cloth from my head. Bunching it in his right hand, he brushed me down the front, clear to my knees, as I knelt on the ground.

My father lit his pipe and began to smoke. After taking several puffs he laid it down and began to sing one of the Chief Medicine Pipe songs. It was the song that is sung while the Feathered Pipe is being unwrapped. He sang it four times, and while he was singing he placed his hands on his sides above the hip bones. After singing, he shook his body from the waist up and coughed lightly. He repeated this act four times.

When he coughed the fourth time, I felt as though something had touched my hands. He asked me if I had felt anything on my hands, and I said yes. My eyes were closed, but he told me to look into my hand, and when I did, I saw a round object there. It was the size of an ordinary marble and it was crystal clear. Inside it I saw the image of a baby. The whole body was red. My father then sang again, and after he had sung four times he again asked me what I saw in my hand. I told him I saw the body of a baby inside of the object, and that it was red. He asked me if I knew what the object was, and I said no.

That object was a hailstone, he said. He took it from my hand and holding it in his own he began to sing again. He sang the song four times, after which he put the stone in his mouth. He told me to open my mouth, then he blew gently into it three times. When he blew into my mouth the fourth time, I felt something going down my throat. I felt it going down until it reached the pit of my stomach, then I didn't feel it anymore. "Now you can go and sit down," he said.

My father told everyone to go home and go to bed, so everyone left and went home, all but White Porcupine and myself. Then my father told me to go home too, so I went, but White Porcupine did not go. I came home and laid my baby down by my husband, and I began taking off my moccasins. I had just taken one off when I heard someone running. I sat down and listened to the sound of the running. It was coming straight towards our tipi. Without coming in my younger sister said, "Sister, come quick, our father is dead."

I jumped up, careless of my bare foot and baby, and ran to my father's tipi. When I entered, I saw him lying there with his clothes off. I stopped and looked at him. I could see that he was not breathing. I ran to him and threw myself upon him. Holding him around the neck I called and called to him, but there was no answer, not a stir in his body. I don't remember what I did next.

When the first shock had passed, my mother told us that Bull Lodge had lain back on his bed and told White Porcupine to wait. "I'll rest a little while, then I'll tell you some more stories," he said. He had raised his arms straight up and stretched himself. He brought his arms down to his sides, then he let out a howl like a bear. When he made that noise, Mother rushed to him and looked at him. He was not breathing. Soon I rushed into the tipi, and as he lay there we could see that there was some live thing in his stomach trying to find a way out. We could see it moving around in there.

That is all there is to tell about my father. He could not exercize the power given to him by the old man with the cane, who gave him four sweat tents which would enable him to rise from the dead. The robes that had to cover those tents could not be obtained, for all the buffalo were gone.

Now I have passed through the experience of living over my father's awful death. I feel relieved that I have accomplished what my father, Bull Lodge, expected of me. I have been very careful not to tell you what I didn't know by filling in gaps with my imagination. There are some things I don't know which are missing from this story. You must remember that I am a woman, and that there are parts of his life he did not tell me about for that reason. But now, although I have suffered greatly in the telling of his life story, I am glad that the voice of my father, Bull Lodge, will always be heard. He died in his eighty-fifth year.

THE STORY OF
THE FEATHERED PIPE

THE STORY OF THE FEATHERED PIPE

This is Bull Lodge's account of the Chief Medicine Pipe known as the Feathered Pipe, as retold by his daughter Garter Snake Woman, aged 73 years. Recorded by Fred P. Gone at Hays, Montana on August 1, 1941.

The story I am going to tell was first told by my father, Bull Lodge, during the time he owned the Chief Medicine Pipe called the Feathered Pipe. One day he gathered his entire family together in the tipi to hear it. Outside of his family, only one person was permitted to listen in on this story, an old man named White Crow.

Bull Lodge's family consisted of his wife, four boys and two girls. My mother's name is One Woman. My brothers are White Porcupine, Otter Robe, Curly Head and Long Hair. My sister's name is Weasel Woman. My grandfather is High Crane and my grandmother is Cook Kill, who belongs to the Frozen Clan.

At this time my father, Bull Lodge, said: "I am about to tell you the story of this Medicine Pipe, which I am bound by tradition to impart to you, my children. Someday one of you will have to remember this story exactly as I tell it. One of you will be called upon to tell it. So I command you all to listen to me, my children, and faithfully remember these things I am going to tell. Then when one of you is called upon to tell the story of this Pipe, you will do so without error."

Bull Lodge began telling this story early in the night and he finished at just about sunrise. My younger sister did not stay to hear the story out. If the owner of this pipe had more than one child, he was obliged to choose one of them to be his Pipe Child. My father chose me as the Chief Medicine Pipe Child when I was four years old. I cannot remember the ceremony performed upon me to give me that title.

It is now clear that it was my destiny to tell this story, just as my father told us it would happen, on the night he delivered it to us. Before I begin, let me strengthen myself so that I may avoid error in the performance of my duty.

Garter Snake Woman then knelt down and crossed herself and held her hands together before her in supplication. She prayed to the Creator to bless her with the spirit of truth, so that she might not be misled. She asked that strength and courage be given to guide her. She prayed that in whatever she said, it would be recognized that the words are not hers, but those of the teller, Bull Lodge.

Her husband (Jim Shortman) and I also knelt down, and we offered a short prayer on her behalf. This old Gros Ventre woman has become almost totally blind. But she possesses a keen memory. She is among those who rarely speak of these things any more, because of the teachings of her present faith. The contents of this story are thus everything we will have. What is not here is lost forever.

The Origin of the Feathered Pipe

A certain man who was forty years old had two wives and two children, a boy and a girl. The spring after he became forty, he had a dream, the contents of which are unknown. He would have the same dream every spring at that time for four consecutive years. In the fourth dream he was told, "Now that I have spoken to you four times, you are to prepare for the coming event." The man then called together the prominent men of the tribe and told them of this dream and its message. Then they spoke in gratitude: "We are glad that at last we are to be given life."

He ordered his lodge to be pitched on the west side of the camp outside of the circle, with the tipi facing east, towards the place where the sun rises. The lodge was richly equipped inside. Besides what his relatives brought in contribution, there were horses picketed nearby. When all was prepared he ordered his youngest wife to go to her parents along with the children and remain there until later.

It was almost summer. All the leaves and blossoms were out, and thunderstorms were in evidence.

He and the older wife entered the lodge. He told his father to advise the people to stake down their tipis, for there would be a terrific thunderstorm that night. He and his wife kept to themselves the rest of the day. Toward late afternoon or early evening, the whole western sky became a solid mass of black cloud. As it approached, the lightning was seen playing in the clouds. A storm came, and it rained almost all night.

Early the next morning, the people were awakened by the man appointed to keep watch. He told them to look where the lodge had been pitched. It was gone, along with everything in it. Even the horses staked out by it were gone. There was only the man and his wife sitting on the ground where their lodge had been. They were facing east, towards where the sun rises, the man sitting at the left side of his wife. (In all the ceremonies of the Feathered Pipe, the position of the man and wife as they sat there has been preserved.) The head of each was covered with a robe, and they sat on a white buffalo robe.

The man had four articles in his hand: the Feathered Wand, the Pipe, the Whistle and the Image.

These objects were wrapped in a material that could not be recognized by anyone. Nor were the articles themselves recognized as belonging to any earthly material. I do not know what they were made of. Just as the white robe had been placed there mysteriously, the four objects were not of this earth. Also, there had been no rainfall where the tipi had stood. The ground was dry for a certain distance around. But everywhere else there was evidence of the night's heavy rain. Water was still standing in the lowest spots and many of the tipis had blown down. Out of respect for their deep faith, no one spoke to the couple. The people remained expectant, knowing that he or she would speak to them in time.

But the man and wife remained sitting on the white robe. The man was naked except for the robe drawn over his head and the four articles in his hands, and his wife was thinly dressed with the robe over her head. Since all their belongings — the lodge, the inside furnishings, the bedding, everything they had, including the horses that had been staked out — were nowhere to be seen, the man's father ordered his own lodge to be taken down and pitched in the same spot.

Sage was picked and laid as a mat inside this lodge, with the tops of the sage pointing toward the center. Then the lodge was fully equipped, with the bed placed in the back directly opposite to the entrance. When this was done, the man and his wife moved back onto the bed which was behind them, but without rising. During all this the man and wife did not speak a word. He kept holding the mysterious articles in his hands and their heads remained covered.

About mid-day the man finally spoke. "Relatives, I have received something for you and my people. This is life, and it will be with our people throughout all generations to come."

"I was given this Feathered Wand, this Pipe, this Whistle, this Image, and names for my wife and myself. I am to be called Man Whistles, and my wife is to be called Woman Goes First." Then they uncovered their heads. The woman took the white buffalo robe they had been sitting on before they moved to the bed, and she spread it out between them, lengthways. The man laid the Feathered Wand, the Pipe, the Whistle, and the Image upon the white buffalo robe, placing them cross-ways so that the Feathered Wand pointed towards the entrance, out to the sunrise. The woman took the end of the white robe on her side and covered the sacred articles. Then the man did the same, taking the end of the white robe nearest him and also covering the articles. This way of covering has been continued ever since. After this was done, Man Whistles ordered a sweat tent to be made, saying, "I will sing in the sweat tent."

Instructions for the Sweat Tent Ceremonial of the Feathered Pipe

These instructions were given to Man Whistles for preparing the sweat tent. Cut sixteen willows and use them to build the tent. Pick sage and place it inside for a mat. Dig a hole in the ground inside the sweat tent and pile the dirt outside, far enough from the tent to leave space for the fire. Pile the dirt in pyramid fashion. Then get sixteen rocks and build a fire between the sweat tent and the dirt pile. Put the rocks in to heat, then cover the sweat tent with robes right to the ground, leaving the front raised to where the tent faces east.

When the rocks were hot enough, Man Whistles was summoned. He got up and walked out of the lodge, going to his left and completing a circle. Then he walked out to the sweat tent and stopped in front of it. Then Woman Goes First rose and picked up the sacred bundle of things wrapped in the white buffalo robe. She tucked them under her left arm and went out the same way her man did and stood beside him.

Then Man Whistles went into the sweat tent, turning to his left upon entering and going to the back of the tent and sitting down. Woman Goes First entered the same way her man did. After reaching the place where he sat, she turned facing the entrance with the bundle still under her left arm. Then she laid it down on the sage mat, with the Feathered Wand pointing to the entrance, facing east to where the sun rises. Now the heated rocks were placed in the hole in the ground inside the sweat tent. A container was filled with water and brought in, made from the paunch of a buffalo and shaped and dried for use as a pail. Then a dipper was brought in for use in pouring water on the rocks, made of a mountain sheep's horn.

Then those who were to take part in the sweat ceremony entered. One man was chosen to pour water on the rocks. The robes on the outside of the sweat tent were lowered to the ground so that it was air-tight. Man Whistles ordered the chosen man to pour a small quantity of the water from the skin container, using the mountain sheep horn dipper to pour it. Then Man Whistles began to sing. He sang a particular song once through, then he ordered more water to be poured on the rocks. He sang the same song once again. After each time the water was poured, he would sing it once through. This was performed four times.

After this he ordered the robes on the outside of the tent to be raised a little while, then lowered again, and the same performance was enacted as before. Water was poured on the rocks, then the song was sung. This was performed four times, and then the robes were raised on the outside. This was all repeated until the robes had been raised on the outside four times. Then the ceremony was done.

Finally all who took part went out. The bundle in the white robe, or the Pipe as it is called, was taken out by Woman Goes First and returned to its place in the back of Man Whistle's lodge. Man Whistles was told that this sweat tent ceremonial was to be performed four times, once each day. This represents the four times he was told in a dream to prepare for this gift, for he had dreamed this once a year for four years. This bundle or Pipe was always to be connected with this sweat tent ceremony. Man Whistles ordered a sweat tent to be made again the next day, and the ceremony was performed exactly as it was the day before.

That second night when Man Whistles slept he had a dream. In it the following instructions were given to him. "Under your pillow you will find some sweet pine, which is to be used as incense in the Pipe ceremonies at all times. As the four consecutive sweat tents represent the first four dreams before the Pipe was given, they also mean that the Pipe will be kept by each individual in four year terms. If at the end of the first four years, the owner is not ready to pass it on, then he is to keep it four years more, and so on, but he cannot keep it more than twenty years."

On the third day when the sweat tent was erected, he used the sweet pine incense for the first time. And he sang a different song, which was sung four times. After each ceremony was over, Man Whistles was the last person to leave the sweat tent.

On the fifth night as Man Whistles slept he was told that when he woke up he would find the ground already prepared directly behind the fire place, which is usually in the center of the lodge.

"You will find a dug-out hole about six inches long, two inches wide and two inches deep, at the tipi's center. It will face the entrance of the lodge and point east, to where the sun rises. Half of the hole is painted black and the other half is painted red. The red half points east to the sunrise and the black half (pointing to the back side of the lodge) means the west, the direction from which the thunder storms come. You will also find a buffalo chip directly behind the dug-out. That is for burning, using the sweet pine on top for incense."

Man Whistles was told that this next sweat tent was the last, and that his final instruction would concern it.

The Fifth Sweat Tent Ceremony

These instructions were given to Man Whistles for the fifth sweat tent ceremony.

Put up a small pole with all the limbs trimmed off except at the top. Leave some limbs at the top of the pole and stand this pole to the east side of the fire, at a safe distance from it. The sacrifices must be hung on this pole, one just below the limbs, the next a little under that, the third still lower down, and the fourth still lower, at the bottom. These sacrifices must be of cloth, and they must be blackened in spots with charcoal. A small bunch of sage must be tied with each piece of cloth which is used for sacrifice.

This pole must stand next to an earth pile shaped in pyramid fashion east of the fire. Thus the pole stands east of both the pile and the fire. A pipe must be placed against the earth pile in an upright position, the stem pointing up. But it must lie along its slope, and placed on the west side of the pile. Thus the stem will be pointing towards the top of the sacrificial pole and the sacrifices. Leaning against the east side of this pole will be a buffalo skull. Its nose will point east, and black circles must be painted around the holes for ears, eyes and nostrils.

When those who are to take part in the fifth sweat tent ceremony have entered the tent, assign the man who pours the water to go outside, taking the pipe with him from the pile. He is to say this after you while standing there: "Above White Man,[1] come and sweat," "Four Old Men, come and sweat." Then call the Pipe owner's name, then his wife's name. After that, you will call out the names of all who are in the sweat tent.

The person you assign to do the calling of the names outside must stand with his head bowed, holding the pipe before him with both hands, the pipe turned slightly up as he repeats the names after. The act of calling Above White Man means calling God's attention to you on earth. The Four Old Men represent the four changes of life.[2] The act of holding the pipe before one and slightly up represents truth. It is the same as an oath. Any single article offered as a sacrifice must be held that way.

1. This is a condensed form of the phrase, "One Above the White Man." The Trickster was often called White Man or Spider. (GHC)
2. The four ages are the feebleness of youth, adolescence, adulthood, and the feebleness of old age. (GHC)

After Man Whistles awoke the next day, he told everything that had been revealed to him in his dream. To fulfill the conditions of the ceremony, he ordered the fifth sweat tent to be built as directed, and he did all the things as he was instructed. That is how the sweat tent ceremony, with all the duties attached to it, was completed at the time of its origin. Ever since then the Feathered Wand, the Pipe, the Whistle, and the Image have been called the Feathered Pipe.

Adding Gifts to the Medicine Pipe Bundle

Man Whistles lived to the age of eight-four years before he was told to place the Feathered Pipe in other hands. During these years he was commanded in dreams from time to time to make an article and add it to the collection. Thus one night he was told to make a drum. It was to be one of those now called a tom tom, a small affair made ten to sixteen inches wide rim to rim. This drum was to be painted around the rim with a rainbow and colored red, black, yellow and white. In the center of the drum surface there should be a picture of a bird, its wings open, with lightning as two streaks from its head. When the drum is finished and ready for use, he was told to use sweet pine, first at the cardinal points on the drum, then holding it straight up above the drum, as the fifth point. When he is to use the drum stick, he is first to make three motions as if to hit the drum but not touching it, then on the fourth motion he is to hit the drum, using it along with his singing. After this, Man Whistles called together the prominent men of the tribe and told them about the drum and its purpose. He told them the drum was to control the thunder. "It is to be used by men when severe thunderstorms come," he said. "I am to use the drum and sing the special song for that purpose, so that storms can pass over quietly."

Another time he was told in a dream that since he had two children, a boy and a girl, he should choose the girl to be the Chief Medicine Pipe Child. He was told that this title would be held by a child in the family wherever the Feathered Pipe made its home, and was to be kept throughout Gros Ventre history. The Pipe owner was to call the Pipe his son and the Chief Medicine Pipe would be the big brother of the Pipe child.

In his next instructions he was told to make a container, something like a parfleche. He was to use rawhide about ten inches wide by twenty-eight inches long, folded back to make it twelve inches long with a four-inch lap for the cover. Each side is sewed with long buckskin strings that also answer for fringes. In this container he was told to keep the smaller articles, such as the small muskrat skin, paints and rattle. He was also told to pick wild parsnip roots, grind them up fine and tie them in a small bag, which was always to be kept in this container. Another time in his sleep, he was told to have an elkhide tanned and used for the outside cover of the Pipe. The hide should be trimmed down to make all four edges straight, with the skin longer one way than the other. Out of the same elk skin he was to cut seven strips of skin about two inches wide by four or five feet long, to be used to tie the pipe when bundled. Then Man Whistles was told to gather birds' feathers of every kind he could get, and tie them into the bundle with a skin thong.

One time Man Whistles was told to get a piece of wood to make a bowl, about six or eight inches across the top. He took a piece out of a tree trunk which might be called a wart, or burl. But he was at a loss as to how to hollow it out. He tried every way he could think of without success. He finally tried using a very rough stone and scraping, but progress was so slow, he knew it would take too long to finish. In despair he laid it on a small buffalo robe on the ground at the head of his bed. He covered it with the tanned elk skin, then lay down on his bed and began to sing, then he fell asleep. He had a dream. Before he began to sing, he had prayed, asking to be shown how to make the wood hollow. In his dream he was told to paint the elk skin. He was to mix red paint in the bowl, blending water and paint. He was to paint the corners of the elk skin with the wet paint, but the balance of the skin was to be painted on both sides with dry paint. When pouring the water into the bowl for mixing, he was to use the dipper made from the mountain sheep's horn.

Now nothing was said about the piece of wood he had put under this elk skin. When Man Whistles awoke he felt desperate regarding the bowl, as he had been ordered to use it for mixing paint although he had not yet been able to hollow it out. He took the elk skin off the piece of wood he had placed under it before he fell asleep. There, to his relief, he saw the piece of wood already hollowed out to perfection. The bowl was finely finished and of expert workmanship. It was painted with dark red paint. Inside, below the rim, a complete rainbow circle was painted. The top color was black, the one beneath was red, the one below that was yellow, and the bottom color was white. Now that the wooden bowl was mysteriously finished, he set about mixing paint for the elk skin, to have it ready as instructed for the outside cover of the Medicine Pipe.

He was told to take the bird feathers he had collected, place them next to the Medicine Pipe on the elk skin, and roll them into a bundle. He was to tie the bundle with the elk skin strips and use them for hanging the Medicine Pipe well above the ground in the lodge. Man Whistles then constructed a pole tripod to support the Medicine Pipe when it is taken outside. When not in use, the tripod is to be placed at the foot of his bed, fastened to one of the lodge poles. The ends of the tripod, where they are tied to the lodge pole, are used to hold the rawhide container (with the rattle, paints and medicine) as well as the little drum and wooden bowl.

After the first four years of keeping the Medicine Pipe, Man Whistles' term was up, but instead of being told to give it into other hands, he was told to keep it one more term. This was done five consecutive times, making it twenty years in all. When the twenty years were up, he was at a loss as to how to proceed and whom to give it to. Then he was told to keep the Medicine Pipe until it was revealed that the time had come to give it into other hands. He was told that he was to keep it until he fully understood the regulations and how to use the Pipe. So the same process resumed, of four year terms at the expiration of which he was told to continue to keep it four more years, until the second twenty years passed, and then he was told to give the Medicine Pipe to his nephew.

Man Whistles was eighty-four years old at this time. He was an old man, and in the forty years of keeping the Medicine Pipe he had become fully experienced concerning it. He kept all his experiences clearly in mind, as he had been told to do, but especially all that took place when he was alone in his tipi on the night he was first presented with the Feathered Pipe.

One night in a dream he was told that before he placed the Medicine Pipe in other hands he was to be given one more thing. During the night a terrific thunderstorm broke and as he slept he was told to look outside in front of his tipi. When he awoke in the morning he looked outside and found, just to the left of the tipi entrance, the promised gift. There were four round balls of hail, he discovered, cased in something that could not be recognized. The nearest people came to identifying it was that it looked like the stuff from which bees make their honeycombs. It was the same color, the size of a small bowl. The round balls of hail were each about a half-inch in diameter and brightly colored, one red, one blue, one yellow and one white.

Man Whistles brought them into the tipi and examined them. As he fingered the hailstones, he noticed that they did not melt but kept their size, and were cold as ice. He made small buckskin bags for them, putting one in each bag. Then he placed them in the large rawhide container where he kept the smaller articles connected with the Medicine Pipe.

That night in his sleep he was instructed about the hailstones. He was to use them to paint the faces of those who were to become owners of the Chief Medicine Pipe. There were sticks for applying the paint, he was told, and the paint and sticks were to be used only when the Pipe is given into other hands on its transfer. So in the morning when he awoke he took down the rawhide bag and opened it. In each of the small bags with a hailstone, he found a small stick, to be used as a pencil for applying the paint. He was told that the paint and stick were to last for all time. (The wood the sticks are made from is unknown, and they never rot.) When Man Whistles picked up the round colored balls in the bags, they crumbled into a fine dust. The hailstones had miraculously turned into paint, still of the same bright colors as when he had found them. He was told to paint faces with them. These last articles that were given to Man Whistles were given on the fortieth year of his keeping of the Medicine Pipe.

One night in the latter part of the winter, he was given his final instructions for the transferring of the Medicine Pipe into other hands. First he was told that on the day he was to act, there would be a rainfall, as a cleansing before the ceremony. He was told that when he transferred the keeping of the Medicine Pipe to his nephew, he would also be conferring supernatural powers upon him.

"There shall be three others in the future who will receive supernatural powers besides your nephew. Thus there will be four persons in all who will receive them during the life of the Chief Medicine Pipe called the Feathered Pipe. Counting from your nephew, the sixteenth man who receives the Feathered Pipe will also receive the supernatural powers which you will confer on your nephew's person, and so on until the next sixteenth man, and the next after him, making four who will have received it." (My father, Bull Lodge, was the fourth man to receive the supernatural powers.)

Since the Feathered Pipe was given to Man Whistles during a thunderstorm, he told his nephew that he would hear and understand the thunder, that he would always know whether the thunderstorm would be mild or severe. And at times the thunder would convey messages to him.

Then Man Whistles told his nephew to follow in his own footsteps, and that he was to keep the Feathered Pipe for sixteen years before he could transfer it. Even then, if he did not receive the word to give it away, he was to keep if four more years, which would make twenty years in all.

Man Whistles was told that when the time came for him to transfer the Medicine Pipe he was to gather a crowd and surround the nephew's tipi. Then all were to enter and take the nephew and his wife by surprise, putting each of them on a robe and carrying them out of their tipi with their heads covered. They were to be taken just as they were found in bed (meaning not dressed for the day) and carried to Man Whistles' tipi. The contents of the Chief Medicine Pipe were to be unwrapped and ready for the ceremony, during which time the singers were to be singing the special song for this purpose.

Instructions for the Ceremony of Transfer of the Feathered Pipe

These instructions were given to Man Whistles concerning the ceremony by which the Chief Medicine Pipe was transferred to his nephew.

The song of the Medicine Pipe must be sung sixteen times. Then you shall make incense with the sweet pine. Incense the whistle, then blow on it four times while standing. The fifth time, blow the whistle with your face up. After you have blown on the whistle, you must paint the faces of your nephew and his wife. First apply the paint to the man, then to the woman. Cover the whole forehead, temple to temple, with dark red paint. Then paint the lower jaws, but do not connect this with the paint on the forehead. Then, with a finger with paint on it, draw a line across the face just below both eyes and around the nose.

The nephew is then to stand up, and while another song is sung by four men whom you shall select, he is to dance with the whistle. Then he is to sit down, and you shall sit down in front of him. Taking the Feathered Wand, you shall proceed to perform the ceremony of conferring the supernatural powers on him.

With the wand in your right hand, make motions as if to place it against his right shoulder, but draw it back before touching him. Do this three times. On the fourth motion go all the way and touch his shoulder with the wand. Next you must do the same to his left shoulder, except that the number of times you gesture to his shoulder is only two, and the third time the wand must go all the way to his shoulder. Then do this again to his right shoulder but only once do you gesture without touching him, and on the second time place the wand on his shoulder. Then go to his left shoulder, and place the wand without gesturing but directly touching his shoulder with it.

While you are performing this upon your nephew, you should pronounce these words of consecration: "My nephew, I confer upon you the supernatural powers that are attached to this Chief Medicine Pipe, that were given to me from above. I command you to use them carefully and discretely in the best interests of yourself and your people."

At this point in her telling, Garter Snake Woman stopped and again offered up a prayer asking for guidance.

"Above White Man, have mercy on me and send me your help, so that I may not make any mistakes. Now I am about to tell the most difficult part. Give me strength so that I do not falter in my words, so that I can control myself and not say anything which is not true.

"I am poor and my intentions are to live a clean life for the rest of my days on earth. Once more I ask you, Above White Man, to help me in my work." Then Garter Snake Woman added, "Now if there is anything missing that you think should be told, bear in mind that I do not know it, otherwise I would tell it." And she resumed her account where she had broken off, at the conferring of power upon Man Whistles' nephew.

Now you must repeat the ceremony with the wand, and during this the Medicine Pipe song is to be sung, but only four times now. Then take the Whistle, and perform the same ceremony upon your nephew with it. Then tell your nephew this: "Now, my nephew, you will always hear from above that which is connected with the powers I have given you." Then take the Image and the Pipe, and perform the same ceremony in turn with each of them as with the Wand and the Whistle.

Next, after performing these instructions concerning the ceremonies of transfer to your nephew, turn to your nephew's wife. Do everything just as it was done to your nephew, except that your wife, Woman Goes First, is to do the talking and conferring of powers upon the niece while you perform the ceremony. Woman Goes First will say to the niece, "I give you power and life. You are to use the powers in the best interests of your people and conduct yourself as befits a woman in your position as Medicine Woman. Respect and honor your husband. Keep yourself free from shame and let no other man touch your person while you hold that position. Always bear in mind the sacredness of what is being bestowed upon you."

How Man Whistles Completed the Transfer of the Feathered Pipe to His Nephew

After the nephew and his wife were taken out of their tipi, it was torn down and all of their property was taken away. (This practice has continued every time the Medicine Pipe has been transferred, except that after the first four times it was moderated.) The property and tipi were then distributed among those who took part in the ceremony. After the ceremonies were completed concerning the transfer of the Medicine Pipe, they gave the nephew a new home. They pitched a new tipi and fully equipped it. Man Whistles was the first to enter. He was followed by his nephew, then by the niece, and then by Woman Goes First, who stood at the extreme left of the entrance.

Now Man Whistles was to perform the last of the ceremony. "My son the Feathered Pipe is changing hands," he said. "Here is where his home is to be. Look down from above and see him and his home." Man Whistles then told his nephew, "Your son the Feathered Pipe must choose his own father four consecutive times." (He meant that the Medicine Pipe itself would reveal the person who is to own it until the fourth man, who must choose the man who will keep the Pipe.) Thus it happened that from the time of the fourth keeper, men would ask for the honor to have the Feathered Pipe in their possession. Once in a while some would receive the message to receive it in their dreams. When it occurred to them in that form, they would patiently wait until the message was given the fourth time before announcing it publicly. Then a messenger was sent to the home of the Chief Medicine Pipe, telling the owner that someone was ready to receive the Feathered Pipe, that it was told to him in dreams four times, which is the customary number.

After Man Whistles finished instructing his nephew concerning the Chief Medicine Pipe which he named the Feathered Pipe, he cautioned him concerning the Pipe and what is expected of him while it was in his care. "My nephew, you are now a medicine man and you are blessed with the supernatural powers that are attached to the Chief Medicine Pipe. You must be very careful how you conduct your behavior. Keep the respect of your people by using your powers properly whenever you are called upon to practice them.

"Do not interrupt the progress of the life of the Chief Medicine Pipe by instituting any ceremonials not given to you by the Medicine Pipe. Always bear in mind the sacredness of your position. Don't make yourself look foolish to the people by overdoing your position among them. Abide by the rules which I have taught you in the handling of the Medicine Pipe and ponder them in your heart at all times.

"Live a solemn life. Pray unceasingly that you do not err in the course of your life, so that when you have finished your appointed term as father of the Chief Medicine Pipe, you may enjoy the fruits of your good work for the rest of your days. From now on, my nephew, you will hear from above what to do. The Medicine Pipe will always guide you until he is ready to be transferred, as he has reserved the right to choose four men who are to keep him."

The Second Man

Man Whistle's nephew kept the Chief Medicine Pipe for five consecutive terms of four years, which made twenty years all together. At the expiration of the twentieth year, the Feathered Pipe told the nephew that the time had come, that the Medicine Pipe must change into other hands. I do not know the names of any of these persons, other than those of Man Whistles and Woman

Goes First. So I will call the nephew Second Man and the keepers who follow him, Third Man, Fourth Man and Fifth Man. When the time had expired for the nephew or Second Man's keeping of the Medicine Pipe, he sent a messenger to Third Man, telling him that he was chosen by the Medicine Pipe to be its next father. Third Man was already aware of his appointment, since it was also revealed to him in his own dream, and he was ready to receive the Pipe.

The same things happened as when Man Whistles transferred the Medicine Pipe to his nephew. It rained first, then Third Man's tipi was surrounded at dawn and Third Man and his wife were taken by surprise. Singing accompanied the performance of the ceremonies. The bundle was opened, uncovering the Wand, the Pipe, the Whistle, and the Image. Then Third Man and his wife were newly clothed. Second Man blew the whistle five times, then he painted the faces of Third Man and his wife. He applied the four articles—the Wand, the Whistle, the Pipe and the Image—to Third Man's shoulders, and a different song was sung for this. Second Man pronounced words of consecration upon Third Man, then Second Man's wife did the same for Third Man's wife. The words were about the same as those spoken by Man Whistles and Woman Goes First, which I have already related. Then the articles were tied up in the bundle again, and there was a procession to Third Man's new home. As they stood before the new tipi, Second Man breathed on the tipi and the Feathered Pipe. The Medicine Pipe was hung above the entrance, and the four persons (the two couples) entered. Second Man instructed Third Man on the use of the incense for the Pipe, and offered parting words and good advice.

The Third Man

After Third Man had received the Chief Medicine Pipe, he lived a pious life and was sincere in his office as a Medicine Man. He seldom ventured out, but devoted his entire time to the Chief Medicine Pipe. He put his whole mind and heart into the keeping of his son the Feathered Pipe.

Third Man would sit for long spells at a time in his tipi and ponder the situation. Sometimes he would sit up far into the night and make incense and think, "I wonder how I'll have to go about transferring the Medicine Pipe and when." Then he would pray to his son the Medicine Pipe and ask for strength to be able to persevere to the time when he must pass it on. One night the Medicine Pipe spoke to him, saying, "My father, don't think of my transfer until I have stayed here for four days (which meant, four years). I'll tell you what to do when the time comes."

After he had received this message from his son the Medicine Pipe, Third Man lived a very quiet life, up until the end of the fourth year. In the late spring of that year, when the first thunderstorm came, he had a dream in his sleep, and the Medicine Pipe told him, "After you have kept me for sixteen years, you are to transfer me to the hands of a certain man" (naming him, but I will call him Fourth Man). "He is to be my next father."

Now that Third Man had learned who was to receive his son the Medicine Pipe from his hands, and knew exactly how long he was to keep it, he devoted the remaining twelve years to caring for the Medicine Pipe as well as he was able. When the sixteenth year came to a close, Third Man was expectant. One night when spring had come, when the leaves were finally out and everything was in full bloom, Third Man had a dream. In it the Medicine Pipe told him, "This coming day is the time for you to transfer me to the fourth man I have chosen." In the Meantime, Third Man had sent a message to Fourth Man that he was chosen by the Medicine Pipe to be its next father and to keep it in his possession. Fourth Man was overjoyed and expressed his gratitude for being chosen by the Feathered Pipe.

That night it rained, which signified the cleansing process at the beginning of the ceremony of transfer. At dawn, Fourth Man's tipi was surrounded and he was taken by surprise. While he and his wife were being carried out of his own tipi, and while he still had his head covered with a robe, he heard someone singing and the sound of that voice was above them. Then the customary rites pertaining to the transfer of the Chief Medicine Pipe were performed by Third Man and his wife upon the persons of Fourth Man and his wife. The ceremonies were identical to the three preceding ceremonies performed in the transfer of the Medicine Pipe.

The Fourth Man

Now Fourth Man had become the father of the Chief Medicine Pipe. He put all his mind to the position he now held among his people and set his heart to the task of keeping the Medicine Pipe in public respect. He would sit and think and silently pray. "My son, I wish you would tell me how best I could serve you. Help me to follow the rules correctly so that I make no mistake in my duties as your father."

Each night he would get up and make incense for his son, the Medicine Pipe, imploring it to make him strong against evil temptation and praying that he might always do the right thing as the father of the Chief Medicine Pipe. One night after sitting up late, when Fourth Man had fallen asleep, he had a dream. "In the morning when you wake up," he was told, "get right up and go to that high hill and wait."

When Fourth Man awoke, without a word to anyone he took up his robe and left the tipi. He looked around for the particular hill he was to go to. This hill was described to him in his dream. Its top was the most bare of grass of any hill around. As soon as he saw the hill, he went directly to the top. Facing east, he sat down and covered his head, humbling himself with resignation to the will of his Maker. Fourth Man remained in that position throughout the day. In contemplation and prayer he exerted his mind and heart to the single purpose of being a good father to his son the Medicine Pipe.

When mid-day came, he felt himself moving, although without effort on his part. He was moving, and when he stopped he knew he was facing south by the heat of the sun in his face. After this experience, he prayed all the harder, never uncovering his head but continuing to sit in that same position. In the late evening as he was sitting there he again felt himself moved. He was turning to the right without any effort of his own. He knew that he was facing west. It was as though he were following the course of the sun. It was not long then until the sun went down and twilight came. Then he heard a voice from above him saying, "You can go home now."

Fourth Man uncovered his head and stood up, letting his robe drop to the ground. After looking around and finding the direction of camp, he picked it up again. But before putting it on he gestured as if to put it on three times, then the fourth time he put it on. Then he did the same thing with his right foot. He gestured as if to step by moving his right foot ahead, then he drew it back. He did this three times, and on the fourth time he stepped ahead and began walking. Thus he came down from the hill and returned to his tipi, and by that time night had come.

When he sat down, his wife was going to give him a drink of water, but he refused it. He took down the wooden bowl (the bowl which had been hollowed out miraculously, now one of the relics attached to the Medicine Pipe). Handing it to his wife, he told her to put it outside just to the left of the door of his tipi. Then he took down the little drum and began to sing. Soon his wife heard sounds as if it were raining. Fourth Man went through the song four times, then he told his wife to step outside and bring the bowl in. She did as he instructed, and handled the wooden bowl very carefully as she brought it in to him. There was water in the bowl, and four wild turnips. These turnips were already peeled, but the peelings were still fastened at the top of each plant, and they were evenly cut into four separate parts. The wild turnips were evenly spaced in the bowl, so that the peelings hung over the rim outside, out of the water.

She placed the bowl before Fourth Man, and he took out the turnips and set them aside. Then he took up the bowl of water and gestured three times as if to drink, but drew the bowl away from his mouth each time. Then the fourth time he brought the bowl up to his mouth and drank all the water that was in it. Then he took one of the wild turnips and broke off a small piece. He went over to where the Medicine Pipe hung and placed it on the Pipe, saying, "My son, I give you a piece to eat." After this he sat down and ate all of the turnips.

This took place at the close of the time Fourth Man was designated to keep the Medicine Pipe, which was twelve years.

The night after Fourth Man's experience on the hill and the miraculous gift of food and drink after fasting, his son the Chief Medicine Pipe came to him in his sleep and spoke to him. "It is now time for me to be transferred to Fifth Man, who is the last one whom I am to choose as my father. Now the designated number of times that I reserved as my privilege of choosing who is to keep me has expired, and I am choosing this Fifth Man because he wants to be my father."

In the meantime Fifth Man had been notified in a dream that he was to become the next person to keep the Chief Medicine Pipe. And in that dream he was told that he was to be blessed with a long life. So he said, "I am glad that one so poor as myself is fortunate enough to be chosen to hold a position that is connected with the

121

Chief Medicine Pipe, and to enjoy a long life." Nevertheless he was a little afraid of the office. But when he received the message to prepare himself for it, he gained confidence in himself and announced that he was ready to take it. As usual it rained for the cleansing, before the ceremony of the transfer was performed.

The next morning Fifth Man's tipi was surrounded and he and his wife were taken by surprise. Then the customary ceremonies were performed as I have described at the beginning of this account. After all the ceremonies were properly performed in Fourth Man's tipi, Fourth Man stood up and took the bundle containing the Medicine Pipe in both hands and began to talk to it. "The four times that you were to choose your place of abode and who was to be your father are accomplished. I am the last one to perform that ceremony. Hereafter, it shall be done according to rules that you have laid down for us. But from now on the man who keeps you must make the choice of whose hands are to receive you. That last rule shall be followed always." Then, turning to Fifth Man, he said, "From now on the Chief Medicine Pipe will be kept by one person from four to twelve years at a time."

After saying these things, he led the procession to Fifth Man's tipi, and standing before it he spoke again. "My son, you who are called the Feathered Pipe, I have served you faithfully, like those before me. I now pass you into the hands of Fifth Man, knowing that I carried you through the time I kept you without fault. The ceremonies you taught us will become history, a tradition that will never be lost to my people for all generations to come. This tradition shall be remembered as long as life exists on this earth."

After saying this, Fourth Man breathed on the tipi and on the Feathered Pipe. He entered the tipi and performed the ceremonies of incensing. When he had finished all the proper ceremonies, he returned to his own lodge.

APPENDIX: GARTER SNAKE AS PIPE CHILD

The following account of Garter Snake as Pipe child (from *The Gros Ventres of Montana: Religion and Ritual* by John M. Cooper and Regina Flannery[1]) provides an informative perspective on her personal relationship to the Feathered Pipe.

There was always, too, a Pipe child—a girl, unless the keeper had no daughters, in which case a son could be selected by him as Pipe child. Thus the oldest son of Sitting High, who had no daughters, became Pipe child. The Pipe child was not necessarily appointed at once by the keeper on assuming the keepership. Garter Snake was not made Pipe child until she was about six years old. Iron Necklace who had been Feathered Pipe keeper some years before her father's keepership was the one who was asked to "confirm" the appointment of Garter Snake [ritual details not obtainable by us] and was given a good horse for performing the ceremony.

The Pipe was addressed and spoken of as the child of the keeper and co-keeper, and they looked upon themselves as the father and mother of the Pipe. When the Pipe talked to them in their dreams it addressed them as "father" and "mother" respectively. To the Pipe child, the Pipe was brother. The Pipe was very jealous, and wanted to be the lone child and so all the keeper's children except the Pipe child were supposed to be put out of the keeper's lodge. According to Garter Snake, however, her father's other children slept in his lodge, not however with the keeper and co-keeper but in separate beds. Garter Snake herself when very young slept with her parents, but later on a separate bed near the foot of theirs. Al Chandler when he was a little boy used to stay with his grandfather, Sitting High, then keeper. The latter would make a bed for the boy right under the Pipe—"which usually was not allowed, but he did it

1. *The Gros Ventres of Montana, Part Two: Religion and Ritual* by John M. Cooper, edited by Regina Flannery (Washington, D.C., Catholic University of America Press, 1957), pp. 133-136.

because I was an orphan, and he would pray that I would be healthy, live to old age, and everything like that. He did that every night as long as I was there."

If a new keeper happened to have a young wife with an infant, they were sent to another lodge.

Some of the activities, duties, and attitudes of a Pipe child can be gathered from the following account by Garter Snake of her own experiences.

"When I was the Pipe child, whenever my mother took the Pipe bundle outside of the lodge, I took the tripod out after her. I was told how to set the tripod when the camp was about to move, with two of the legs close together and the third far out. Whenever my father made smudge with pine needles, he would give me some and I would chew them and would hold my hands over the smudge. Then I would rub my left palm up my right arm, my right palm up my left arm, then both palms from the top of my head down the sides of my neck and down my breast.

"I did not have any duties beyond helping my mother when she brought the Pipe bundle out and brought it in.

"I was forbidden to pick peppermint. If peppermint was mixed in dried pounded meat, I was not allowed to eat the meat. If a coyote or wolf were killed, I was not supposed to touch it. These were the only two prohibitions I was under.

"If anybody vowed to be painted by the keeper, I would be present at the rite next to my mother and sit there through the ceremony.

"Whenever while I was the Pipe child I got sick my father would put pine needles on me, and then he would take down the bundle and put it on my parents' bed, and would say to me: 'Put your arms around your brother [the Pipe] and pray to your brother so you may get well.' The Pipe keeper and his wife claim the Feathered Pipe as their son and tell their children that the Pipe is their brother. When I put my arms around the Pipe I was told to say to the Pipe: 'My dear brother, have pity on me, that I may get well of my illness.'

"Of course the Pipe was not human but because I was a baby when my father got it I grew up with it and thought just as much of it as of my own blood relatives. When my father transferred the Pipe to Sitting High I was outside playing. When I was coming home I saw the bundle at Sitting High's door, and when I saw it I started to cry, and when I saw my father I said to him: 'Why did you give my Pipe away?' It was just like a person leaving. I was lonesome for it, and felt just as if I had lost a relative or friend. And all through my life I have felt the same toward it. All through my life I have made it a point to be present at any Feathered Pipe ceremony. And whenever I went to any ceremony, I would bring something for it. Since I joined the Catholic Church I stopped doing this, but even now I feel: 'It's all alone. I pity it.'

"When while I was Pipe child I had been out playing and in the evening would come home and see the Pipe bundle over the door, I would stand and look at it a long time and would say: 'Feathered Pipe, I am going into our lodge now.' Once when I was sitting on the bed in the lodge I got to thinking, and all the folks were there, and I said: 'Feathered Pipe, my dear brother, look down on me and watch over me.' I was not told to say this, and I do not know what made me say this prayer to the Feathered Pipe.

"My father used to tell me: 'This Pipe was given by the Supreme Being through Bha'a, the Supreme Being is the father of the Pipe.'"

CPSIA information can be obtained
at www.ICGtesting.com
Printed in the USA
LVHW020312270822
726951LV00001B/150

9 780803 272569